# THE 72 NAMES OF GOD

# THE 72 NAMES OF GOD

## Technology for the Soul

BY YEHUDA BERG

www.kabbalah.com™

For further information:

The Kabbalah Centre
155 E. 48th St., New York, NY 10017
1062 S. Robertson Blvd., Los Angeles, CA 90035

1.800.Kabbalah
www.kabbalah.com

First Edition
May 2003
Printed in the USA
ISBN 1-57189-135-8

Design: Hyun Min Lee

## DEDICATION

For יהושע Josh

May The 72 Names of God give you the power to be your best self.

## ACKNOWLEDGMENTS

I would like to thank the many people who have made this book possible:

First and foremost, Rav and Karen Berg, my parents and teachers. I will be forever thankful for your continual guidance, wisdom, and unconditional support. I am just one of the many whom you have touched with your love and wisdom.

The great Kabbalistic masters: Rabbi Shimon bar Yochai, Rabbi Isaac Luria, Rabbi Yisrael Baal Shem Tov, Rav Yehuda Ashlag, and Rav Yehuda Brandwein. Without these great souls and their commitment to spreading the word of Kabbalah, none of us would have the opportunity to study today.

Michael Berg, my brother, for your constant support and friendship, for your vision and strength. Your presence in my life inspires me to become the best that I can be.

My wife, Michal, for your love and commitment; for your silent power; for your beauty, clarity and uncomplicated ways; you are the strong foundation that gives me the security to soar.

To David, Moshe, and Channa, the precious gifts in my life who remind me every day how much there is to be done to ensure that tomorrow will be better than today.

Peter Guzzardi for helping to make the power of the 72 Names real and accessible to everyone who needs it.

Billy Phillips, one of my closest friends, for your help in making this book possible. The contribution you make to The Kabbalah Centre every day and in so many ways is appreciated far more than you could possibly know.

Camila Olson, Ruth Zilberstein, Mitch Siskind, Hyun Lee, and Esther Sibilia, whose contributions made the physical quality, integrity, and accessibility of this book live up to its spiritual beauty and heritage.

Bruce Bobbins, Nancy Spiegel, and David Lipke, our team at Dan Klores Communications Inc. for their understanding, vision, and effort in bringing *The 72 Names of God* to the world.

Phillipe Teman and David Shamouelian at Sharagano, for making *The 72 Names of God* part of this season's collection and part of your life.

Christian Witkin, who is gifted with the ability to capture people in their most favorable Light.

To my two special friends who introduced me to jujitsu and encouraged me to change my eating habits so that I can reinforce my spiritual health with physical nutrition; you are a true inspiration and I love you both very much. You know who you are.

To Marcus Vinicius, my jujitsu master, for all your patience and support.

Sometimes people who affect you in extraordinary ways come into your life. To my amazing friend - thank you for coming into mine.

Thank you to my friends at all the Kabbalah Centres worldwide—you are a part of me and my family no matter where you may be.

The students of The Kabbalah Centre—your desire to learn, to improve your lives and share with the world is an inspiration. The positive changes I see in all of you every day makes everything I do worthwhile.

**PART THREE**

**FOREWORD**

In the pages of this book, you will find a set of supremely powerful spiritual tools, an entire technology of healing, protection, and positive change. Yet for 3400 years this technology lay hidden in the letters of three biblical verses, each containing 72 letters. These verses describe the miraculous parting of the Red Sea before the people of Israel, as they fled bondage in Pharaoh's Egypt. As you are about to discover, the mystical power of the Hebrew letters that parted those waters can likewise part whatever Red Sea now confronts you in your own life. In fact, I can say without exaggeration in these pages you will find not just another technology or an advanced technology, but all technology—whether of the 21st century, or the 30th, or the 50th—for the elimination of chaos from your life.

The revelation of these letters after many centuries is itself a miracle, one that was accomplished only in the past 80 years by the great kabbalists Rav Yehuda Ashlag and Rav Yehuda Brandwein. Through their work, the technology of the 72 Names of God has become available to everyone, together with the knowledge of how to activate that technology and manifest its benefits in our daily lives.

Let me emphasize the fact that the 72 Names are intended for all humanity. Like the words of the Bible and the Hebrew letters that comprise them, the Names are the property of no ethnic group or religious identity. They can and should be used by everyone to confront the accelerating chaos and negativity that afflicts our world. Indeed, if they are not used, only disappointment, frustration, and despair can result. With this in mind, it astonishes me to realize that in all my years of traditional religious studies, I was never made aware that this technology even existed. From earliest childhood I had read and re-read the verses containing the 72 Names, but I never knew of the combinations of letters that were hidden in those verses or of their unique powers. And I was certainly not alone in lacking this awareness. In this book, therefore, you will very quickly gain knowledge and capabilities that had been denied even to scholars who had devoted their lives to study and explanation of the sacred writings.

In Yehuda's book a great power awaits you. As you begin to explore this power and put it to use, I would like to emphasize two points. First, the 72 Names are a technology for asserting the power of human consciousness over physicality. That is, the power of mind over matter, which Kabbalah has always understood and which science is just now beginning to grasp. However, the Names themselves depend on your individual consciousness, and on your commitment to what the kabbalists call proactive behavior. This is another term that I had never heard until I began studying Kabbalah, yet it's the foundation of the whole technology of the 72 Names. What is proactive behavior? First and foremost, it is a stepping back from reactive impulses, for there is no way we can have consciousness of God—to say nothing of God's consciousness—unless we step back. Without this proactive behavior, even this most powerful of all technologies cannot possibly work for us. Whenever it seems that misfortune has suddenly been thrust upon you, step back. This does not mean acceptance of the circumstances—if someone slaps you in the face, you might indeed hit them back—but it does mean a level of consciousness above mere reactivity. The technology of the 72 Names can and will work for you, but not without proactive behavior.

My second point is related to the problems caused by reactive impulses, specifically difficulties related to ego. In the biblical text that is the foundation of the 72 Names, ego is personified by the Pharaoh of Egypt. As the ego-driven impulses in our own lives draw us away from growth and transformation, Pharaoh gives the Israelites their freedom, but then changes his mind and sends his army after them and ultimately into the waters of the Red Sea. Ego will always play this game, particularly if we make an effort to be proactive. Once again, step back from this impulse. Be aware that your normal state of being in the physical world is reactive consciousness. We are always being called upon to play ego's game. With the ego it is always lose-lose situation. If we are concerned with winning, that's ego. If we are concerned with losing, that's ego too. Using the 72 Names helps us to move beyond the ego's game.

When you commit yourself to proactive behavior and to the renunciation of ego games, the technology of the 72 Names is truly within your grasp. Very simply put, this is the power of mind over matter. This is the ability to eliminate every kind of chaos, whether in the form of intangible fears and negative emotions, or the all-too-tangible challenges of cancer and other serious illnesses. Consciousness is the power that underlies every action and event in the material world. Whether it is the simple act of raising your arm or the spontaneous healing of life-threatening disease the process begins in consciousness. The 72 Names of God are the bridge between this power of consciousness and its manifestation in the physical realm. May you use them to gain the beautiful, wonderful miracles that await us now and in the future for yourself and for all humankind.

Kabbalist Rav Berg

THE 72

## PREFACE

**Do not accept any of the lessons or wisdom presented in this book blindly or on faith alone.**

Test everything you learn. Review The 72 Names of God and apply their knowledge and their power in real life. Tangible results should be your only yardstick when measuring the potency of this book.

NAMES

OF GOD

*All of you . . . who see land beyond the horizon, who read sealed, hidden missives and books, who seek for buried treasures in the earth and in walls, you who teach so much wisdom, such high arts—remember that you must take unto yourselves the teachings of the Kabbalah if you want to accomplish all this.*

—Paracelsus, one of the founding fathers of Western medicine

Okay. So things haven't been exactly great lately.

In fact, if you're being honest, you've been miserable, on and off. But perhaps most disturbing, the usual quick fixes are showing signs of not working anymore. The late nights at work, the shopping binges, stuffing yourself with rich food, overdoing the drugs or booze, the relentless effort to control your environment—or to let it all go. Nothing you've tried fully suppresses the gnawing feeling that life isn't turning out the way you'd thought. You may have the job you always wanted, the mate, the home, the clothes, the car, the kids —or you may have none of the above. But one thing is for sure: the things you counted on to bring you happiness just aren't doing the job.

How do I know all this? Because I've been there myself, and I see it in so many people who come to The Kabbalah Centre, looking to make a change in their lives.

What if I could provide you with a simple set of spiritual tools, proven effective for over 4,000 years, that could lift you out of the garbage of your everyday life? Putting them to work might not be quite as easy as buying a pair of shoes or popping a pill, but it's not a whole lot harder either. And there's no buyer's remorse, no hangover. The side effects are nothing but good. All you need is some information you don't have now.

Incidentally, when I refer to spiritual tools, the spirituality I'm talking about has nothing to do with remote mountaintops, or golden rays of sun piercing cloud-covered skies. It might be found in a given church, or temple, or mosque, or yoga center, but then again it might not. The important thing is that it's an active, practical spirituality, designed to reach right into the garbage where you are now and pull you out. Rather than describe it any further at this point, I'd like you to read a story that conveys a sense of how it works far better than I can. It's a contemporary version of a tale passed down from one generation to another for centuries . . .

PART ONE

When we identify and work to transform our self-centered qualities and crooked characteristics, the key turns and the gates unlock. Blessings and good fortune are now free to rain down upon us.

Ike the mail carrier lived in a small town in the Midwest. He and his wife Cathy had only one child, a son named David. When David turned seven years old he was stricken with a mysterious illness. With each passing day, the young boy grew weaker. Ike drove hundreds of miles to visit countless doctors but to no avail. Cathy could see in her baby boy's eyes that time was running out. She could sense the angel of death hovering over his bedroom. Little David desperately needed a miracle.

It so happened that a wise old man lived in the same town as the mail carrier. He was not a doctor, but local people came to him with ailments that resisted a cure; it was rumored that he could talk to angels and perform all kinds of miracles and wonders. Ike's last option was to pay a visit to the old sage.

When he learned of young David's heartrending situation, the wise man was greatly saddened. Ike begged him to do something in the way of prayer and blessings. The healer took Ike's hand in his, and promised to do the best he could.

That night the old mystic ascended high into the spirit world, utilizing secret prayers and other worldly meditations known only to a few. When he reached the gates of heaven he was stunned to find that the gates were locked. The fate of the little boy had already been sealed.

The night soon passed and the morning sun began to rise in the eastern sky over this quaint Midwestern town. Ike and the old sage met outside the post office in the early morning. Sorrowfully, the old man told the mail carrier the news.

"I'm afraid there is nothing I can do", the sage said. "It has already been decreed that the gates of heaven remain locked to your only son."

Ike was shattered. Tears began streaming down his face as he begged the old man to try one more time. "I have nowhere else to turn!" cried Ike. "David is my only son, my only child. And you are my only hope!"

Not having the heart to say no to this broken man, the old mystic replied, "I cannot promise anything. But I will make one more attempt."

And that's when a bizarre idea suddenly occurred to him. He quickly summoned his young assistant, Thomas, and made a peculiar request. "Please go at once to the nearest city," the mystic said, "and bring to me ten hardened criminals. No less than ten."

Thomas was shocked. But he knew better than to question the man who could talk to angels.

"Find me pickpockets, burglars, looters, the worst scoundrels possible," the old man added. "And please, hurry!"

Thomas drove into the city and, to his surprise, he was able to gather together ten thieves quite quickly. In fact, he was amazed at how easily they agreed to accompany him to the home of his master. Even these villains had heard of the mysterious healer in the not-so-distant town who possessed supernatural powers.

Thomas and this sordid band arrived at the house of the mystic. The wise old sage thanked them for coming and invited them all into his home. Some of the nastiest criminals in the state sat around his living room, boastfully recounting their favorite crime stories. Then the old man motioned for them to be silent. Something about him commanded their respect. So they all listened carefully as the mysterious old sage who could perform miracles, the healer who could cure the most dreadful ailments, asked each one of these wily thieves to assist him in what would be his most difficult, most impossible miracle of all!

The next morning, at the break of dawn, as robins chirped and roosters crowed, as a sweet-scented summer breeze blew ever so gently, Ike the mail carrier was dancing wildly down Main Street, looking like the happiest man on earth.

A car pulled up alongside the dancing Ike. Thomas was at the wheel. In the back seat was the old sage. "My dear friend," he exclaimed, "It appears by your delightful face and your dancing shoes that you have good news to share."

"I thank you with all my heart!" cried the mail carrier. "My beautiful boy David received a miracle overnight. It's as though he was never sick. He is out milking the cows right now, doing chores as we speak!"

"Indeed, this is very good news," said the man who could talk to angels. "Be well, my friend!" The old sage then drove off.

Thomas was puzzled. He turned to his mentor in the back seat. "How can this be?" he asked him. "You're a gifted healer. But those men I brought to you yesterday . . . they were burglars, safecrackers, and muggers. Thieves. Why did you not ask for God-fearing, upstanding citizens? Why did you pray with such shady characters?"

And this is what the noble and kind sage told him:

"When I prayed that first night for our friend and his only son, I saw that the Gates of Heaven were locked. There was nothing I could do. The poor man's heart was shattered. How could I refuse him when he pleaded with me to try again? Then a thought came to me. So I asked you to bring me that assortment of villains, which you did. Then last night I prayed again, but the gates of heaven were still locked."

Thomas was confused. "So what happened?" the driver asked. "How did you cure Ike's son if the gates remained locked?"

The mystic then cracked a smile that bespoke great wisdom. "Ahhh, but this time I had a band of thieves to assist me." He replied. "You see, Thomas, a good thief knows all about breaking and entering. They picked the locks! These criminals broke into heaven and that is how my prayers were able to sneak into the heavenly sanctuary."

The car continued on into the small town the sage called home. It was still early, but the streets were coming to life. And if you knew where to look you would have seen a number of professional criminals, intermingled among the honest townspeople, suddenly stop and discreetly tip their hats to the healer's car as it passed by.

This simple story is actually a profound metaphor that contains the greatest formula in the world to getting all of your prayers answered:

The Formula:

- The mystic in this story symbolizes our own soul, all of our positive character traits.

- The thieves represent all of our negative and egocentric traits. After all, we are all thieves, to one degree or another.

Our good nature and endearing qualities will not arouse the answers to our prayers. Rather, it's our mischievous, dishonest attributes that provide the master keys to heaven. When we identify and work to transform our self-centered qualities and crooked characteristics, the key turns and the gates unlock. Blessings and good fortune are now free to rain down upon us.

## THE OLDEST WISDOM

Although the spiritual tools I'm talking about don't require anything more than momentum provided by you to swing into action, it's helpful to know that they come from a venerable spiritual tradition called Kabbalah. In fact, Kabbalah offers the oldest wisdom in the world, tracking back more than 4,000 years. It began with Abraham, the father of three great monotheistic religions: Judaism, Christianity, and Islam. Abraham recognized that there were two spheres that affect our lives: spiritual and physical. He revealed the laws for both of these spheres—which is to say, a code of laws for the workings of the entire universe. He explained how the spiritual world intersects with the physical world, and what we can do at that intersection to create happiness.

Using these laws of the universe, Kabbalah offers a system that explains all of the real-life issues that keep us stuck in the garbage. This has tremendous value. If you don't know how gravity works, you might attempt a great leap and injure yourself; without some knowledge of electricity, you might put your finger in a socket and get a bad shock. Understanding how things work can help you; not understanding can hurt you. Ignorance is the reason bad stuff happens; Kabbalah provides the antidote.

Science, physics, biology, religion, spirituality, and philosophy all have their roots in Kabbalah, like branches on a tree that emerge from a single seed. Kabbalah profoundly influenced the greatest thinkers of history, including Abraham, Moses, Jesus, Mohammed, Pythagoras, Plato, Newton, Leibniz, Shakespeare, and Jung. That's pretty impressive—especially when you consider that most of the world has remained oblivious to the existence of Kabbalah throughout the ages. This is due to the secrecy that surrounded Kabbalah as well as its complexity, which made Kabbalah difficult to understand and to share. A new generation of Kabbalists is dedicated to making the benefits of Kabbalah accessible to everyone. This book is one expression of that commitment.

Kabbalah profoundly influenced the greatest thinkers of history, including Abraham, Moses, Jesus, Mohammed, Pythagoras, Plato, Newton, Leibniz, Shakespeare, and Jung.

It's like turning on the light in a dark room. These forces empower us to completely change our lives and absolutely transform our world.

## CRACKING THE CODE

Perhaps the most remarkable aspect of Kabbalah is its long-hidden connection to the Bible.

Kabbalah says the Bible is a complete code. That's right. It's a cryptogram. When this biblical code is cracked, something wonderful happens: awesome spiritual forces are suddenly released into our souls and discharged into the world at large. It's like turning on the light in a dark room. These forces empower us to completely change our lives and absolutely transform our world. But when the Bible remains coded, read and taken literally (as it has been for some 2,000 years), it becomes a fruitless symbol of religious tradition instead of the awesome instrument of power it was meant to be.

A prime example of a highly charged, encoded story in the Bible is the account of Moses and the Israelites parting the Red Sea . . .

## THE MEANING OF A MIRACLE

Let's go back in time, some 3,400 years ago. Here's the situation:

Six hundred thousand Israelites are stranded on the banks of the Red Sea. Pharaoh and the ferocious Egyptian army are in hot pursuit of the Israelites, hell-bent on killing those who resist and returning the rest to slavery. The Israelites are cornered. There's nowhere to go. They either drown in the sea or face Pharaoh's chariots. It's not much in the way of options.

They need a miracle. Fast. So they cry out to God the Almighty, the all-merciful Master of the Universe, the Creator of the cosmos. They beg for help. And what does the Creator say in response to their cries?

"Why are you calling out to me?"

Not exactly the kind of response one might expect from an infinitely compassionate Creator. But this is, in effect, what the Bible, the Torah, the Old Testament says was God's response. And if that's not enough, the next response from God is even more baffling.

"Go jump in the water!" the Creator tells these poor suffering souls.

How does a rational person make any sense of this?

Enter Kabbalah.

According to Kabbalah, a tremendously powerful technology is encoded and concealed inside the biblical story of the Red Sea. (You'll find it in Exodus, Chapter 14.) Three verses tell this story—19, 20, and 21—and each verse contains 72 letters.

The following charts reveal how the 72 Names are derived from the biblical text. Keep in mind that this is the first time in human history that this secret is being revealed publicly.

## HOW TO DECIPHER THE 72 NAMES OF GOD FROM SCRIPTURE

Take the first letter of the first box (which is ו), and the first letter of the second box (which is ה), and the first letter of the third box (which is ו) and guess what? You now have the first secret Holy Name of God that appears in the first box, top right, of the chart.

Pretty easy right?

Now, for the second Name, you simply take the second letter of the first box (which is י), the second letter of the second box (which is ל), and the second letter of the third box (which is י), and voila! You now have the second Holy Name of God that appears in the box immediately to the left of the first box.

If you follow this simple pattern for all the letters in the three verses, you will unlock the most powerful and most ancient technology for achieving control over yourself and your life.

וַיִּסַּע מַלְאַךְ הָאֱלֹהִים הַהֹלֵךְ לִפְנֵי מַחֲנֵה יִשְׂרָאֵל וַיֵּלֶךְ מֵאַחֲרֵיהֶם וַיִּסַּע עַמּוּד הֶעָנָן מִפְּנֵיהֶם וַיַּעֲמֹד מֵאַחֲרֵיהֶם:

God's angel had been traveling in front of the Israelite camp, but now it moved and went behind them. The pillar of cloud thus moved from in front of them and stood at their rear.

| | | | | | | | | |
|---|---|---|---|---|---|---|---|---|
| מ | מ | ע | א | שׁ | ל | א | ו | 1 |
| ד | פּ | ע | ז | ר | פּ | ל | י | 2 |
| מ | נ | מ | ר | א | נ | ה | ס | 3 |
| א | י | ו | י | ל | י | י | ע | 4 |
| ו | ה | ד | ה | ו | מ | ם | מ | 5 |
| ר | ם | ה | ם | י | ו | ה | ל | 6 |
| י | ו | ע | ו | ל | נ | ה | א | 7 |
| ה | י | נ | י | ר | ה | ל | ר | 8 |
| ם | ע | ן | ס | מ | י | ר | ה | 9 |

וַיָּבֹא בֵּין מַחֲנֵה מִצְרַיִם וּבֵין מַחֲנֵה יִשְׂרָאֵל וַיְהִי הֶעָנָן וְהַחֹשֶׁךְ וַיָּאֶר אֶת הַלָּיְלָה וְלֹא קָרַב זֶה אֶל זֶה כָּל הַלָּיְלָה:

It came between the Egyptian and the Israelite camps. There was cloud and darkness that night, blocking out all visibility. All that night [the Egyptians and Israelites] could not approach one another.

| 8 | 7 | 6 | 5 | 4 | 3 | 2 | 1 |
|---|---|---|---|---|---|---|---|
| ה | כ | ל | ה | ל | י | ל | ה |
| ק | ר | בּ | ז | ה | א | ל | ז |
| ה | ל | י | ל | ה | ו | ל | א |
| שׂ | ר | ו | י | א | ר | א | ת |
| י | ה | ע | ג | ן | ו | ה | ו |
| י | שׁ | ר | א | ל | ו | י | ה |
| ו | בּ | י | ן | מ | ו | נ | ה |
| ו | ג | ה | מ | צ | ר | י | ם |
| ו | י | בּ | א | בּ | י | ן | מ |

## Third Verse

וַיֵּט מֹשֶׁה אֶת יָדוֹ עַל הַיָּם וַיּוֹלֶךְ יְהוָה אֶת הַיָּם בְּרוּחַ קָדִים עַזָּה כָּל הַלַּיְלָה וַיָּשֶׂם אֶת הַיָּם לֶחָרָבָה וַיִּבָּקְעוּ הַמָּיִם:

Moses extended his hand over the sea. During the entire night, God drove back the sea with a powerful east wind, transforming the sea bed into dry land. The waters were divided.

| | | | | | | | | |
|---|---|---|---|---|---|---|---|---|
| י | ה | י | י | ה | ו | ד | ו | 1 |
| ב | י | ל | ם | י | ל | ו | י | 2 |
| ק | ם | ה | ע | ם | ר | ע | ט | 3 |
| ע | ל | ו | ז | ב | י | ל | מ | 4 |
| ו | ז | י | ה | ר | ה | ה | ש | 5 |
| ה | ר | ש | כ | ו | ו | י | ה | 6 |
| מ | ב | ם | ל | ז | ה | ם | א | 7 |
| י | ה | א | ה | ק | א | ו | ת | 8 |
| ם | ו | ת | ל | ד | ת | י | י | 9 |

## Complete 72 Names Chart

| | | | | | | | |
|---|---|---|---|---|---|---|---|
| כהת | אכא | ללה | מהש' | עלם | סיט | ילי | והו |
| הקם | הרי | מבה | יזל | ההע | לאו | אלד | הזי |
| וזהו | מלה | ייי | נלך | לוו | פהל | כלי | לאו |
| ושר | לכב | אום | רוי | שאה | ירת | האא | נתה |
| ייז | רהע | וזעם | אני | מנד | כוק | להוו | יוז |
| מיה | עשל | ערי | סאל | ילה | וול | מיכ | ההה |
| פוי | מבה | נית | נגא | עמם | הועש | דני | והו |
| מומי | עמו | יהה | ומב | מצר | הרוו | ייל | נמם |
| מום | היי | יבם | ראה | וזו | איע | מנק | דמב |

The energy that drives this ancient technology comes from these three verses and their 72 letters. The 72 Names of God are not "names" in any ordinary sense. They have nothing in common with what you and I call ourselves. The 72 Names of God provide us with a vehicle to connect to the infinite spiritual current that flows throughout reality. God gave this cutting-edge technology to Moses to be shared with all people, so that humans could unleash their own God-like powers and attain control over the physical world.

When God asked the desperate Israelites, "Why are you calling out to me?" it was merely code. God was actually telling the people that they *themselves* had the power to escape from their perilous predicament *on their own*. They did not need God's assistance.

In fact, God never answers prayers. It is people who answer their own prayers by knowing how to connect to and utilize the divine energy of the Creator and the God-like force in their own souls.

How's that for a complete paradigm shift?

The miraculous power to get out of any life-or-death situation—then or now—can be found in this ancient technology known as the 72 Names of God.

Now follow this next idea closely. When God told the Israelites to jump into the sea, it was also a code revealing the actual technique for activating the power of the 72 Names!

It works like this.

To seize control over the laws of Mother Nature one must attain self-mastery.

Most of us are aware of the outcome of the literal Red Sea story: just before the Egyptian army reached the Israelites, the Red Sea parted and the Israelites raced off to freedom. What a miracle! But Kabbalah reveals that it wasn't God who parted the sea. It was Moses. And he used the power of the 72 Names of God to engineer this amazing feat.

What's more, *before* the waters rose to the sky, a physical action was required to activate the power of the Names. *This is the secret meaning* behind God's response of, "Go jump in the water."

The Israelites were required to demonstrate total certainty in their God-like powers, and in the 72 Names, by physically walking into the sea with complete conviction in a positive outcome.

Naturally, when they first stood by the banks of the sea, watching Pharaoh fast approaching, they were gripped by fear and doubt. But then Moses reminded them of the 72 Names. They began meditating upon them, employing all their mental powers to arouse breathtaking spiritual forces.

But you know what? Not a single water molecule moved until the Israelites conquered their doubts and waded into the sea with total certainty. Not one drop shifted until they were neck-deep in the sea. Then, when the waters reached their nostrils, and they *still* maintained complete certainty—*swoosh*—the waters parted, giving them passage to freedom.

What's the lesson?

To seize control over the laws of Mother Nature one must attain self-mastery.

Therein lies the secret to the 72 Names of God.

But before you can master human nature, you need to know a little bit more about it.

Every possible form of pleasure was included in this Light.

## HIDE AND SEEK

Pretend, for a moment, that you're eleven years old. You're playing hide and seek with your best friends and you're "it." So you lean up against a tree, you cover your eyes with your hands, and you begin counting to ten, slowly.

How would you feel if, after reaching ten, you turned around, opened your eyes, and saw all the kids just standing there, right in front of you?

Not much fun, right? The purpose of the game—having fun and deriving pleasure from playing—cannot be realized, can it? That happiness can be achieved only if all the kids hide. And the better their hiding spot, the more fun it will be!

Well, this is similar to what happened *prior* to the creation of the physical world and physical human beings.

## IN THE BEGINNING

Before the birth of the universe, the only reality was infinite nonphysical energy that expanded endlessly. Kabbalah calls this endless expanse *Light*. Every possible form of pleasure was included in this Light. From the pleasures derived from sex and chocolate, to the heavenly feelings of serenity and pure bliss, *everything* a person could conceive of, long for, crave, or desire was included in this Light of happiness. This was the domain of God the Creator. There was no time. No space. The Creator then created all the souls of humanity for one great purpose: to bestow this infinite Light of happiness upon us.

The Light was handed to us freely. But just like our previous example of hide and seek, it wasn't much fun because everything was simply set down before us, openhandedly. It felt like a free lunch. A handout. Charity. In other words, we were created; we opened our eyes, figuratively speaking; and all that happiness was just sitting there right in front of us.

But something was missing.

## WHAT WAS MISSING

Essentially, the missing ingredient was the pleasure we derive from the *challenge* of playing hide and seek. In other words, our newly created existence would have been even more fun and fulfilling if *we*, ourselves, could create this Light of happiness instead of just receiving it courtesy of the Management.

So we said to the Creator, "Let's play hide and seek! You hide Your Light. We will then find it."

## BECOMING GOD

When we work hard to find the Light, we feel a sense of accomplishment. We feel responsible for our own happiness. We feel like the cause. We feel like God. And nothing, but nothing, feels better than feeling like God, especially when we receive endless happiness as part of the package.

So that's essentially what happened. We closed our eyes, we counted to ten, and the Light hid. When the Light disappeared, this physical and dark universe erupted into existence!

So we said to the Creator, "Let's play hide and seek! You hide Your Light. We will then find it."

## CREATION OF THE WORLD

This Divine act of *hiding the Light* is the cause behind the origins of our universe, which astrophysicists believe was born in a Big Bang. In fact, there are many uncanny congruencies between astrophysics and Kabbalah concerning Creation, as you will see below.

### What Kabbalah Says
*(Based on the teachings of the 16th century Kabbalist Isaac Luria)*

Before the Light hid, there was an exquisite unity. Oneness. No such thing as time and space.

When the Light hid, a point of space erupted into existence, also marking the birth of time.

This occurred some 15 billion years ago (from our reference point).

The point then expanded (think of a balloon being blown up), creating empty space. God emanated a ray of energy into this vacuum. This energy eventually formed all physical matter, including stars, planets, and people.

Four different forces unfolded from the initial state of unity during the process of Creation.

### What Science Says
*(Quoted from physicist Stephen Hawking and PBS's* Stephen Hawking's Universe*)*

> The universe, and time itself, had a beginning in the Big Bang, about 15 billion years ago. The Big Bang marks the instant at which the universe began . . . and all the matter in the cosmos started to expand. Before this time all four fundamental forces—gravity, electromagnetism, and the strong and weak nuclear forces—were unified.

It's the same story, the only difference being that Kabbalah provides a reason why the Big Bang happened, whereas science merely tells you how it happened.

In our hide and seek metaphor, the idea of counting to ten extends the analogy. It actually refers to *ten curtains* that were erected to gradually diminish and thus hide the dazzling radiance of the Light. These ten curtains created ten dimensions, each progressively darker than the other.

Our chaotic physical universe represents the darkest of the bunch.

Now guess what? Two thousand years after Kabbalah revealed that reality consists of ten dimensions, modern-day physics reinforced it with what is known as Superstring Theory.

Today the Superstring Theory is the hottest contender in science's quest to formulate a Theory of Everything.

Check out the similarities.

**What Kabbalah Says**
*(Based on the teachings of the 16th century Kabbalist Isaac Luria)*

Reality consists of ten dimensions. Nine of these dimensions are beyond time and space. Only our physical world contains space-time.

Six of the ten dimensions are actually folded into one.

**What Physics Says**
*(According to Physicist Brian Greene, from his book* The Elegant Universe: Superstrings, Hidden Dimensions, and the Quest for the Ultimate Theory*)*

> For string theory to make sense, the universe should have nine space dimensions and one time dimension, for a total of ten dimensions.

Dr. Michio Kaku, internationally recognized theoretical physicist, writes in his book *Hyperspace:*

> Physicists retrieve our more familiar four-dimensional universe by assuming that, during the Big Bang, six of the ten dimensions curled up (or "compactified") into a tiny ball.

It's remarkable, isn't it?

## WHERE THE LIGHT HIDES

Let's go back to our childhood game of hide and seek for a moment. Suppose one of your friends decided to hide behind a large rosebush. Before you can find this particular kid, you must *first* locate the rosebush. Life works the same way. Before you find the Light, you must first discover the Light's hiding spot.

So the all-important question becomes:

*Where exactly is the Light's hiding spot?*

According to Kabbalah, humans were created with two distinct aspects to their nature—darkness and Light.

The darkness is the human ego—as in:

E<sub>verybody's</sub> G<sub>ot</sub> O<sub>ne</sub>

Bingo! This is where the Light hides.

The Light is the human soul, which is obscured by the ego. You see, the ego is not actually you. You just think it's you. But it's really an external garment, a curtain that hides the Light of your soul, your true self.

To make this game of hide and seek truly challenging, the ego was given full reign, complete dominion over your thoughts and "natural-born" behavior. Your soul, on the other hand, was subdued, *hidden* from your conscious desires, concealed from your rational mind.

Where exactly is the Light's
hiding spot?

EGO

They give you the chance to let go of your ego, selfishness, and envy and in turn, find the Light!

## THE POINT OF LIFE

The purpose of your existence is to allow the full intensity of the Light to shine in your life and in this world. This is called heaven on earth. Whether you're a doctor, lawyer, scholar, plumber, CEO, artist, teacher, carpenter, accountant, entrepreneur, factory worker, engineer, electrician, computer jockey, or rocket scientist, you have two ways to carry out your work and conduct your life:

1. **Through your ego, doubting or oblivious to the truth of the Light, considering only yourself**

2. **Through the humility of your soul, constantly finding the Light and considering the needs of others**

Your career, your family, and your friends are here for one purpose—to provide opportunities for you to carry out your personal transformation. They give you the chance to let go of your ego, selfishness, and envy and, in turn, *find the Light!*

## CURTAINS THAT BLOCK OUT THE LIGHT

Each time you allow your ego to control your behavior in business, marriage, and your relations with other people, another curtain is suspended concealing the Light of your soul and the Light of the Creator. Within this added darkness, your ego grows stronger, your true self becomes more concealed, and life grows progressively darker.

This is called **Reactive Behavior**—you react to the impulse of the ego.

Each time you resist your ego, you tear down a curtain.

This is called **Proactive Behavior**—you stop your reflexive egocentric impulses and unleash the proactive will of your soul. Life grows brighter.

## FREE WILL

Your only *free will* in life is to choose to resist or not resist your egocentric urges. Each time you resist reactivity in favor of behaving proactively, you have exercised free will.

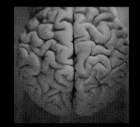

# How do we remove the curtains and blockages?

# Suffering or spiritual transformation.

## LOOKING FOR LIGHT IN ALL THE WRONG PLACES

So now you know! The Light hides behind the ego—and all of its abundant reactive traits. Unfortunately, we have all been socially conditioned to focus on our good traits, our charming qualities, our positive characteristics. We totally ignore, deny, and neglect our dark side.

This is why we have failed to find the Light! We've been looking in the wrong place since the dawn of human existence.

## THE PROBLEM

This is the tricky part: Each time we behave with ego, we block out the Light just a little more. Human existence grows a little bit darker.

Which leads to the million-dollar question:

*How do we remove the curtains and blockages?*

## SUFFERING VERSUS SPIRITUALITY

There are two ways to remove the curtains that obscure the Light of the soul: *suffering* or *spiritual transformation*. That's all. There are no other options.

Let's examine this Kabbalistic notion further.

Our egos diminish from the emotional pain and our souls suddenly blossom.

When we suffer, when we experience pain, when we undergo grief and heartache, the *hurting* actually purges ego and self-interest from our nature. The soul—our true self—shines brighter in that moment. This is why we suddenly feel a sense of love and unity with others when planes crash into buildings and those buildings collapse on national TV. This is why we feel a shift in our priorities when the rubble of human remains litters the landscape as a result of war, terror, or tragic accidents.

Our egos diminish from the emotional pain and our souls suddenly blossom. This is why we run to help others when we're exposed to pain or suffering. And this is why firefighters, police officers, emergency medical teams, and ordinary people suddenly risk their lives to save another human being. This is why we suddenly feel inspired to change the world and ourselves when we confront terror and tragedy. Our true, selfless, divine self shines through whenever our egos are battered and shaken to the core.

## THE EGO STRIKES BACK

So why hasn't the suffering you've experienced in your life left you full of the endless joy that comes with the Light? The problem with suffering as a path to the Light is that, with few exceptions, the changes in the ego are only temporary. Why? Because as the memory of our pain subsides, the ego again tempts us into reacting to its impulses. In turn, our new reactions resurrect the ego's power.

Over time, the ego slowly but surely regains its strength and reclaims control. The soul's influence gradually begins to fade. Your good mood, new priorities, and caring feelings give way to rotten moods and intolerance. Priorities shift from family back again to 50-hour work weeks. Suddenly, you no longer want to change the world. You just want to change your car for one that's nicer than your best friend's. You're back to gratifying your self-indulgent desires. Once again you're staring down people who accidentally bump into you in the shopping mall, or you curse them under your breath. Daily life goes back to being one reaction after another.

*So what are you to do?*

Must you always experience catastrophe just to "wake up" for a short while, only to find your ego lulling you back into a false sense of security?

Fortunately, the answer is no.

## THE TOOLS OF TRANSFORMATION

The 72 Names of God is the oldest, most powerful spiritual tool known to humanity.

It's an ancient technology that is far more powerful than anything we have yet discovered in this 21st century. Why? Because The 72 Names of God functions at the DNA level of the soul, at what physicists call the quantum level of reality.

The 72 Names of God targets the ego; it takes aim at all our nasty traits but from a purely proactive standpoint. You'll learn *how* as you discover the meaning of each Name in Part 2 of this book.

Over time, the ego slowly but surely regains its strength and reclaims control. The soul's influence gradually begins to fade. Your good mood, new priorities, and caring feelings give way to rotten moods and intolerance.

Conflict, intolerance, and darkness cannot, by definition, exist in the presence of Light and true spirituality.

## IT AIN'T ABOUT RELIGION — IT NEVER WAS

You should know that The 72 Names of God is not about religion. In fact, God never created religion. Humans did. And this human-made invention has done nothing but create separation between people. Tragically, more blood has been spilled on behalf of religion than from all other diseases and crimes combined.

Religion fosters hatred. It gives rise to war and genocide—all in the *name* of God. Well, *war, hatred,* and *genocide* are not any of God's names.

The fact of the matter is that divine wisdom, by its very nature, can evoke only harmony between people. The arousal of love and peace is an intrinsic effect of a genuine spiritual wisdom. It naturally builds bridges between people of opposite faiths. It inherently embraces and empowers all people. It is universal, like the universal force of gravity, making no distinction between race, personal beliefs, or personal bank accounts. Gravity doesn't care whether you are black or white, rich or poor, educated or illiterate—if you step off the balcony of a high-rise tower, you'll come crashing down to the pavement.

If a so-called religion displays any form of hostility or division within its own ranks or toward another religious faith, if it doesn't generate Light and provide answers to our most challenging questions 100 percent of the time, then something is terribly amiss. Conflict, intolerance, and darkness cannot, by definition, exist in the presence of Light and true spirituality.

## A LITMUS TEST

By the way, you'll know if a spiritual wisdom is pure and *connected* if, as you learn, you catch yourself saying, "Wow, I already knew this. I always felt these truths somewhere deep inside of me. I just didn't know how to articulate them."

(If you don't say that at least once while reading this book, throw it in the trash!)

The key to this universal law is the offering of *true* Light and *unconditional* kindness.

The power of The 72 Names of God operates strictly on a soul level, not a physical one. It's about spirituality, not *religiosity*. Instead of being limited by the differences that divide people, the wisdom of the Names transcends humanity's age-old quarrels and belief systems to deal with the one common bond that unifies all people and all nations as one —*the human soul*.

The Kabbalists were clear on this matter: You must offer unconditional love and true Light to your friends and even those you see as enemies if *you* want to receive peace and serenity in your *own* life. You must see the soul of the other person and connect to it.

For instance, if a Jew offers unconditional love and shares genuine spiritual Light with a Muslim or a Christian, even if he loathes him, love and Light will be returned to him in equal measure, without fail. It's a natural law.

The key to this universal law is the offering of *true* Light and *unconditional* kindness.

The reason is, *unconditional* love and *authentic* Light immediately penetrate the soul of the other party, awakening love and Light in return.

If that prerequisite is met, all forms of hatred, conflict, and hostility *must* vanish as quickly as a lit light bulb banishes darkness from a room.

If it doesn't happen, then make no mistake, it wasn't genuine Light that was being shared; there was a hidden agenda behind the love that was offered, there were strings attached to the kindness that was given. It wasn't *un*conditional.

If your effort at peacemaking is not 100 percent sincere, if there's a hidden agenda or speck of self-interest, then this kind of *conditional* love never reaches the other person's soul. No love is awakened. In other words, it's merely one ego communicating to another.

So how do you arouse true Light? How do you awaken the soul?

Easy! The same way you bring light to a darkened room.

Simply flip on the switch.

## FLIPPING THE LIGHT SWITCH

The moment your eyes touch the 72 Names of God in the pages that follow, spiritual Light of unimaginable force and brilliance is ignited.

This Light sets your soul aflame. This Light banishes the darkness that is your ego. This Light empowers the *entire* world the moment you decide to share it with all existence. People the world over start experiencing all those wonderful feelings of love, unity, and caring without having to first suffer, merely by your thoughtful meditation on these Names.

This is the promise of The 72 Names of God. Never, ever settle for anything less. Especially when the ego pipes in and says, "This is too good to be true," or "It's too simple to be real."

So exercise your free will! Reject skepticism. Make use of the Names. Meditate that the Light you ignite is empowering your soul and the souls of all humanity. Know with deep conviction that Light and goodness are triumphing over darkness and evil.

And then look around. See if your life is getting better. See if you can spot real miracles taking place in your life and in the world at large.

And keep in mind: Each time you flip a page to a new Name, you flip on another Light switch.


## HEBREW TECHNOLOGY

If you've flipped through the pages ahead, I know what you're thinking: "I can't read Hebrew!" It doesn't matter. Not in the least. This book is not about foreign languages or unfamiliar alphabets.

First of all, the 72 Names of God are not actual words. With a few exceptions, they are not pronounceable in any meaningful way. Their particular configurations are devoid of literal meaning. They are sacred sequences, activated visually.

Second, the Hebrew word for *letter* actually means "pulse" or "vibration."

What's pulsating? What's vibrating? Energy! A flow of energy transfers directly to you when your eyes behold the shapes of the Names.

Third, these universal meditation symbols transcend religion, race, geography, and the very concept of language. The Names were intended for all people, as a global instrument to connect us to the Light. Their power is released through their unique shapes, through the patterns expressed in their lines and curves.

## HOW TO USE THE 72 NAMES

The three-letter sequence that forms each of the 72 Names operates much like a cable transmitting various blends of energy into our physical world.

The three letters signify three forces:

- A positive charge

- A negative charge

- A ground wire

This structure creates a circuit of energy that safely channels spiritual current into your life, just as a three-prong plug securely transmits electrical current into your home appliances.

When you meditate upon these various three-letter sequences, a particular spiritual influence is transmitted directly to your soul.

But there are three prerequisites to activating the power of the 72 Names:

**1. Conviction in their power**

**2. An understanding of the particular influence radiating from each Name**

**3. A follow-through physical action to activate their power**

The first prerequisite is up to you. But know in advance that your ego will flood your mind with doubt and uncertainty. That particular battle is personal and yours to contend with.

Engaging and winning this battle is the ultimate purpose of life. Remember, this is how you find the Light.

The second prerequisite is provided for you. In the pages that lie ahead, the spiritual influence and power of each Name is being made public for the first time in history! Appreciating this fact will further enrich and enhance your connection to the Light.

The third prerequisite is sometimes the hardest one to observe. For instance, if you are using a particular Holy Name to triumph over your fears, you will have to confront the fear in order to eradicate it from your life. It's like a small test, a simple physical action that flips on the "Light switch." But you should know that when you confront it with your newfound spiritual strength, you *will* conquer it, and you'll be well on your way to a life free from fear.

Likewise, if you're trying to eradicate your ego, a physical situation will soon arrive that will inflame your ego just so you can resist it.

FUSION

So, the awesome power of the 72 Names of God is generated by an elegant fusion of spiritual power and a follow-through physical action.

Or you might think of it this way: A man arrives home late one night. His house is totally dark. Obviously, the man desires to have some light on in his home. But the desire is nonphysical, and the electrical current flowing throughout the house is also not physical. To manifest his desire, the man must take physical action. He must walk over to the light switch and flip it on.

A physical act is always required in order to activate intangible forces in our world— whether it's electrical current or the Light of the Creator.

It is this kind of fusion between spiritual and physical that produces all the power of the 72 Names of God.

The three-letter sequence that forms each of the 72 Names operates much like a cable transmitting various blends of energy into our physical world.

Through the letters you can access the Light that is within you—the Light that comes from the Creator.

In fact, they have always existed within you. Now they have been reawakened.

Set aside a few moments in a quiet setting where you're unlikely to be disturbed. Take a seat in a comfortable, straight-backed chair, or sit on the floor if you prefer.

Now think about what has caused you to call upon this power at this particular moment in your life. What Red Sea confronts you? What army of Pharaoh is approaching from behind?

Do you see your present circumstance, however dire it may seem, as an opportunity for revealing Light? If so, terrific! The Light will be revealed through the power of the Names. Or do you simply wish to exchange your current situation for something more comfortable —a quick fix? If so, this present circumstance will surely reappear until you understand things differently.

Ask and answer these questions honestly and courageously. When you're certain that your meditation is grounded in positive choice, look through this book to find the letter sequence that most closely pertains to your concern or aspiration.

Read the text that accompanies the letters. Then simply allow your eyes to rest on the letters with full attention, but without undue focus or concentration. (When meditating on the letters, peruse from right to left.)

It's best not to think of any specific positive outcome you hope to realize. Instead, let your mind become quiet as awareness of the letters fills your consciousness. If you find yourself distracted by random thoughts, try to focus on your breathing—on the sequence of inhaling and exhaling—while your eyes continue to rest on the letters. With each inhalation imagine the power of the letters filling your body with Light. With each exhalation allow the Light to enter you and permeate your entire being.

After a few moments, close your eyes and see the letters in your mind's eye. Imagine them as clearly as possible, just as they were when you were looking at them on the page. See the black letters sharply outlined against a white background. Then open your eyes.

Once again, focus on the letters in the book. Continue this for a comfortable interval.

Now close your eyes and visualize the letters once more, but this time imagine them in white against a black background. Let them occupy your mind as completely as possible. Be aware that the letters are no longer on the page—*they are within you.* They are your connection with a part of yourself that predates your hopes and fears, and even your life. Through the letters you can access the Light that is within you—the Light that comes from the Creator.

When you feel a desire to do so, open your eyes. Avoid the temptation to look again at the letters on the page. For the time being, their existence in the book is irrelevant. They now exist within you. In fact, they have *always* existed within you. Now they have been reawakened.


## THE WRITING OF THIS BOOK

Completing this book has been a very personal and quite unpredictable journey of discovery for me. Let me mention just one unexpected turn in the road that I encountered.

Throughout my life, I was always drawn to the teachings associated with the 72 Names. I was surprised to find, however, that the Names had never been collected and explained in a single volume. References to many of them existed here and there in the Kabbalistic literature, but only in a scattered fashion, and some seemed to have been entirely over-looked throughout the centuries. As a result, I began work on the book you now hold in your hands.

The task was not only more difficult than I expected, but it was difficult in a completely unanticipated way. I was able to find information on many of the Names relatively quickly, but this only made the absence of others seem more and more important. And, like a jigsaw puzzle, the task was an all-or-nothing enterprise. Having 65 or even 70 names was no better than having none at all.

So I spoke with my father and my teacher, Kabbalist Rav Berg, about the problems I was having. I asked the Rav about specific books and authors I should consult, but he surprised me with a much more sweeping statement.

"Just let it go," he said. "If you're not finding what you want, stop looking."

I was puzzled. I had seen the Rav encounter far bigger obstacles and I couldn't recall seeing him just back away. Nevertheless, I let go—and I learned that the advice of a Kabbalist is not always what it seems.

This is a book of power—the power of the mind, the power of the soul, and the power of unseen spiritual forces that permeate our existence.

Soon after, while perusing a Brooklyn bookstore, I noticed a red-covered volume. It looked relatively unworn, but when I opened the book I saw that this was far from true. It had been re-bound in a new cover, but the pages themselves were yellowed and fragile—and in those pages I found the very wisdom I had been seeking. For me, this discovery was confirmation that the book you're now reading was truly an expression of the Creator's Light. It certainly wasn't any conscious intention on my part that led me to that bookstore, and to the volume with the bright red cover. In fact, it was only by following my father's advice to "let go" that my search was completed.

That's the way it has always been in my life. Whenever I have listened to the counsel and wisdom of both my father and my mother, wonderful blessings have come into my life. Their presence in my life, along with the presence of my wife and children, continues to be the greatest blessing I could ever hope to receive.

Finally, it is my wish that you be open to receiving the power of the 72 Names. The benefit from meditating on these Names is far more valuable than all the treasures of the world. The possibilities of the universe we live in are far more advanced than we can possibly imagine.

This is a book of power—the power of the mind, the power of the soul, and the power of unseen spiritual forces that permeate our existence. When these three *power sources* are harnessed and correctly brought together, we acquire the capability to control and positively transform human nature, Mother Nature, and, in turn, our entire world.

Ultimately, then, this is a book of deep personal fulfillment and genuine peace.

It is my deepest hope that you will use this knowledge for the sole purpose of connecting with the Light of the Creator and to share your positive experiences with others.

Blessings and Light!

*Look, if you had one shot, or one opportunity, to seize everything you ever wanted—one moment—would you capture it or just let it slip?*

—Eminem

PART TWO

## TIME TRAVEL

Science says that for every action there is an equal and opposite reaction; for every cause, there is an effect. But in the physical world there is always an interval of time between an action and its result.

*Time is the distance between cause.................and effect.*
*Time is the space between crime.........and consequence.*
*Time is the gap between good deed.......................and dividend.*

The chain of cause and effect could be ten minutes, ten days, ten months, or even ten lifetimes. Nevertheless, the effects of our behavior come back to us in full measure.

We believe, mistakenly, that good is unrewarded, that evil goes unpunished, and that life lacks true justice. Why? Because the memory of our positive and negative actions fades over time, and when their delayed effects appear, we see them as simply random events.

What's more, unkind words also set the cause-and-effect principle into motion.

So, how do we return to the original cause *before* its nasty effects show up in our lives?

The technology for this exists in this unique Name. Long ago, Kabbalists declared that time travel was possible. Today, quantum physicists are catching up to Kabbalah by acknowledging that time travel is achievable, at least in theory. But Kabbalah doesn't say we will *physically* rocket back in time to encounter our own self face-to-face. That's an intriguing concept, but here we achieve an objective far more dazzling than the notion of having lunch with ourselves somewhere in the past. What is that objective? How about unimaginable joy and fulfillment, once we correct all the negative actions of our past?

## MEDITATION

Awaken remorse in your heart for prior misdeeds. Accept the frank spiritual truth that problems in your life are the result of past actions. Concentrating on this Name will *now* uproot the negative seeds you've already planted. In doing so you transform your past, reshape the present, and assure yourself a future full of joy and fulfillment.

# TIME TRAVEL

When we want to undo past "crimes" in order to
banish their painful effects from our lives and the lives
of others, this Name provides us with an ingenious
time travel device. Forget the Dramamine, this flight
happens on a soul level.

Are you ready? Fasten your seatbelt!

## RECAPTURING THE SPARKS

When asked what they want most from life, most people mention the following:

- HAPPINESS
- JOY
- PROSPERITY
- PEACE OF MIND
- WISDOM
- FREEDOM
- ENLIGHTENMENT
- PURPOSE

What do these have in common? We can't touch them. We can't see them. They emit no aroma, nor do they have taste, weight, or color. But according to Kabbalah, all these intangible qualities can be expressed by a single word—Light! Just as sunlight contains all the colors of the rainbow, spiritual Light contains all the "colors" of fulfillment that a human being seeks throughout existence.

This resplendent spiritual Light permeates all reality. But there's one problem. As we've discussed, negative actions can create negative effects. Every day, we consciously or unconsciously react to ego-based desires and instincts. Each *reaction* creates a new negative force that robs us of our Light. These forces are very real, despite what our egos might tell us. These dark entities have no life of their own; they subsist off our energy. We nourish them each time we display selfishness, intolerance, anger, fear, or any other reactive trait. As their power grows stronger, our lives grow progressively darker.

### MEDITATION

Shards of Light are drawn out of the destructive entities that reside within your being. Their life force is cut off and you are replenished with Divine energy. Life grows brighter each and every day as billions of sacred sparks return to their source—your soul!

When we find ourselves stuck in first gear, when our energy reserves are on empty, when we feel like our very life force is slowly being sapped, lost sparks of spiritual Light can be regained and restored in our lives.

# RECAPTURING THE SPARKS

## MIRACLE MAKING

The 72 Names of God were used in ancient times to bring about astonishing miracles. Moses used the Names to part the Red Sea. Joshua employed them to stop the sun, and David called upon them to defeat Goliath. Sadly, however, the power of the 72 Names was lost for millennia—and perhaps the greatest miracle of our own time is the sudden availability of this ancient power.

This sequence of letters pertains to the art of miracle making. But a certain level of understanding is required before the immense power of this Name can be unleashed. We must realize, for example, that mere *information* is not power. A child can be given the blueprints for building a 747 airliner, but that data would be useless. *Knowledge*, on the other hand, really is power. *Wisdom* is power. These inner qualities can be applied and translated into practical, positive change—even miracles!

Any miracle in the material world must be preceded by a miraculous change in our own character. Physical reality and human nature are intimately connected. When we create an extraordinary transformation *within*, the power of this Name allows the universe to *externally* express this inner change.

### MEDITATION

Free yourself from all selfishness, envy, anger, and self-pity. By rejecting these negative temptations, you are also free to invoke this Name—and thereby ignite the power of miracles.

There are times when nothing less than a miracle can transform a bleak and hopeless-looking situation. But God does not perform miracles; we do. The technology for engineering miracles is found within this divine Name.

Go ahead. Make a miracle.

## MIRACLE MAKING

## ELIMINATING NEGATIVE THOUGHTS

Thoughts do not originate from the physical matter of the brain. The brain is merely a radio that broadcasts thoughts to the rational mind. So where does the actual *broadcast* come from?

Kabbalah teaches that there are two distinct sources—the Light Force and the Dark Force. These are like two separate broadcasting stations, and they're on the air 24 hours a day!

Here's the real problem: The Dark Force of ego has control over the airwaves of our mind! Twenty-four/seven, at full volume, negative and egocentric thoughts dominate our consciousness. This Dark Force is the source of all our fears and doubts. In comparison, thoughts that come to us from the Light are barely noticeable. It's only when we manage to tune out the signal transmitting from the Dark Force that we're able to hear the faint sounds of our own souls.

Recurrent thoughts include *uncertainty, constant worrying, dread,* and *excessive fear* to the point where we become ridden with anxiety. Negative thoughts also include those terrible things that we think about other people when they aggravate us. Or those harsh judgments we wish upon others when we envy them.

Obsessive-compulsive behavior also begins with uncontrollable negative ideas. Shutting down our negative mental processes frees the mind and automatically curbs obsessive behavior.

A cold heart is an opening for an onslaught of harmful, unproductive thoughts. When our hearts become open and warm, we seal these openings once and for all.

### MEDITATION

You are now switching off destructive thoughts emanating from the ego. In the space that is then opened, a gentle radiance of spiritual Light floods your heart and mind.

When obsessive thoughts—*worry, anxiety, fear, pessimism, uncertainty, and negative fantasies*—invade us, we can "take our minds back" and focus on thoughts that move us forward, not backward.

עלם

# ELIMINATING NEGATIVE THOUGHTS

## HEALING

Moses became the liberator of the very slaves he had helped to rule. Because of this tremendous transformation, the letters that compose his name hold great spiritual power. This particular configuration transmits the forces of healing.

There are two ways to fully activate this power of healing:

**1. Think about others.**
Meditate on people who also need healing. As the energy of healing passes through us to assist others, we automatically receive the benefits ourselves. The more we share, the more we receive.

**2. Be accountable.**
Without question, this is a difficult step to take. We must lose the victim mindset. We must realize it was something we *did*—in this life or a past life—that brought about illness. Immediate causes such as the foods we eat, or even our genetic makeup, are simply the weapons that inflict illness upon us. They are not the causes, they are the effects. One person smokes four packs of cigarettes a day and lives to a ripe old age. Another never smokes, but still contracts lung cancer. Get the picture?

Blaming someone or something absolves us from all personal responsibility. But if we accept responsibility—100 percent—then and only then will the tools of *The 72 Names of God* arouse the Light of the Creator so we can be healed. (If you're having doubts about this provocative spiritual truth, return immediately to the previous Name and banish all those skeptical thoughts!)

## MEDITATION

The power of this Name brings you the energy of healing at the deepest and most profound level of your being.

Why?

Because you accept full responsibility for your present state and condition! And you concentrate on others who also need healing.

The concept of *sickness* extends beyond illnesses that afflict the body. It includes the "poor health" of a business, an "ailment" in a relationship, and emotional "illnesses" such as anxiety and depression. With the right tool, we can heal all manner of dis-ease.

מרפא

# HEALING

## DREAM STATE

When we fall asleep, the daily chains of physical existence that trap our souls in our bodies loosen. As we slumber, our souls become free to ascend into the spiritual atmosphere where they receive nourishment, power, and the occasional tune-up. During this nightly sojourn, our souls are in a realm beyond time and space. Past, present, and future become one. The full panorama of a human life span is displayed, from birth to death.

Our souls catch sight of future events, both positive and negative. These glimpses are then filtered down to the body, where they take the form of dreams. Dreams contain both lies and truths. If we're spiritual, our dreams are predominantly truthful. If we're egocentric, our dreams will be misleading. These influences affect us subconsciously, impacting the decisions we make in life. The more truthful our dreams, the wiser choices we make. And vice versa.

If we can extrapolate the messages from our dreams and nightmares—consciously and subconsciously—we understand what we have to change about ourselves. Spiritual change is the proactive way to deflect negative effects and judgments that might be heading our way.

MEDITATION

With this Name you dream truthfully. Your soul ascends to safe and loving places during the night. You awake each morning recharged. Reinvigorated. Renewed in body and spirit. Wiser.

# DREAM STATE

According to Kabbalah, our physical universe is not all there is. In fact our world of early morning coffee and traffic jams is just one of many dimensions. These other dimensions are accessible in different ways, one of which is through our dreams.

## DNA OF THE SOUL

Before time began, the infinite Light of the Creator was concealed in order to create a point of darkness, a space into which our universe could be born. The purpose was to build an arena where there was no Light and no order, where we could, through our *own efforts* of sharing and choosing good over evil, create our own spiritual Light.

To conceal the infinite Light, ten "curtains" were erected, each reducing the Creator's Light a little more until a place was created that was almost devoid of Light. This is our world of chaos, of confusion, and of the second law of thermodynamics, which states, among other things, that everything must eventually undergo decay and degeneration —all things must become increasingly disordered. It's known as entropy. (In case you've wondered, that's why it takes about a half gallon of water to cook macaroni, and about a full gallon to clean the pot.)

The 22 letters of the Hebrew alphabet are the instruments of Creation. They are the DNA of our universe and our soul. This Name connects us to the full power of these 22 forces of Creation, which is a really good thing, because it brings renewal, order, and creative power to the areas in which we desperately need them.

## MEDITATION

Here you receive nothing less than the full impact of the forces of Creation. You restore meaning to lives that often feel meaningless, and purpose to a world that often appears aimless. Order returns. Structure emerges. Everything is tidied up.

When life appears fragmented and disjointed, we can create order out of chaos, tranquility out of turmoil, and calm out of commotion by bringing everything back to its original perfect state—back to the DNA of our lives.

We just didn't know it . . . *until now!*

# DNA OF THE SOUL

## DEFUSING NEGATIVE ENERGY AND STRESS

According to Kabbalah, we all have a spiritual field of energy that extends a little more than seven feet from our bodies. Although we can't see this field with the naked eye, it's as real as the invisible atoms in the air, and as undeniable and influential as the unseen force of gravity.

Whenever this field is charged with negative or stressed-out energy, we find ourselves in a lower state of being—suffering from sadness, stress, depression, hostility, fear, and uncertainty. Or we just feel plain miserable. Unpleasant places and gloomy people influence our lives when we come into close contact with them. Our personal space is violated, charged with disturbing energy detrimental to our well-being.

## MEDITATION

Purifying Light banishes unseen ominous forces and deactivates harmful influences lurking nearby, including those that dwell inside you. Stress dissolves. Pressure is released. Balance and positive energy permeate your environment.

# DEFUSING NEGATIVE ENERGY AND STRESS

When we encounter places oozing negative energy; if we come in contact with people radiating darkness, anger, or hatred; when pressure increases, this Name will neutralize any and all negative forces, including stress and nervous tension.

## ANGELIC INFLUENCES

Our senses and consciousness are, by design, limited. Therefore the power of angels remains out of sight to the eye and elusive to the rational mind. But—like the wind, gravity, or radiation—the influence of angels is very real.

Did you ever:

- Accidentally slip and fall for no apparent reason?
- Hit your thumb (instead of the nail) with a hammer?
- Make a really, really stupid decision?
- Experience a losing streak that never seemed to end?

This is the influence of negative angelic forces at work. Good fortune is the result of the influence of positive angels.

Acts and words that embody sharing, tolerance, compassion, and self-control over our ego and its constant stream of judgments ignite positive forces. They also end the existence of negative angels. Behavior that exemplifies selfishness and intolerance creates negative forces.

According to quantum physics, countless subatomic particles are constantly coming in and out of existence in all parts of the universe at every moment. At this microscopic level, these so-called virtual particles can pop into existence for brief moments before returning to nothingness, causing up and down energy fluctuations. This is another example of science discovering the physical counterpart of spiritual reality.

MEDITATION

Using this Name you now access the network of angels. You remove negative angels and their chaotic influence from your life. You ignite the force of positive angels. And all this power is activated by your sincere commitment toward transforming your character.

# ANGELIC INFLUENCES

The universe is seething with both positive and negative angelic forces. Forget those images of cherubs!
In truth, an angel is a *particle* of spiritual energy. Like subatomic particles, angels pop in and out of existence from our words, thoughts, and actions.

## LOOKS CAN KILL: PROTECTION FROM THE EVIL EYE

*A person possessing an evil eye carries with him the eye of the destroying negative force; hence it is called "destroyer of the world," and people should be on their guard against them and not come near them so that they should not be injured by them!*
    —Zohar I, p. 68b

Eyes possess tremendous powers. The human eye has the capability to transmit both positive and negative energy. The *evil eye* refers to the negative glances and resentful looks that we receive from people harboring destructive feelings toward us. Kabbalists attribute much of everyday misfortunes to the evil eye.

By the same token, when we cast the evil eye toward others, we create a greater opening within ourselves, attracting even more negative glances and their accompanying harmful effects. We become more vulnerable as our spiritual defenses are weakened. Thus, the evil eye brings equal harm to both the bearer and the recipient.

### MEDITATION

Your own desire to cast the evil eye at others is diminished. A shield of positive energy surrounds you, offering protection from the negative glances, looks of envy, and mean-spirited intentions of others.

The ancient masters describe this Name as a powerful, invincible weapon of war. It assures victory in the longest and most important battle in human history —the battle against our own evil eye and that of other people.

# LOOKS CAN KILL: PROTECTION FROM THE EVIL EYE

## BANISHING THE REMNANTS OF EVIL

When we move into a new home or a new place of business, any negative activity by the previous occupant affects us. Evil and negativity leave a residue. These leftover dark impressions dramatically impact our lives when we're in their presence. We can even feel them at a table in a restaurant if the previous customers were extremely unpleasant people.

When everything is going wrong at home or at work, evil residue is frequently the concealed culprit.

Life is chaotic and frantic enough as it is. No one really needs additional fiendish powers derailing their day-to-day endeavors.

This Name purifies places and spaces where evil, wickedness, and spiritual darkness linger.

## MEDITATION

All negative forces are expelled from any places in which you dwell. The Light of this Name deactivates negative energy and cleanses your environment.

If we feel our skin crawl, the hairs on the back of our neck stand on end, or an uneasiness as we enter a place, it's usually the result of negative forces in our midst. This Name neutralizes those forces.

## BANISHING THE REMNANTS OF EVIL

## UNCONDITIONAL LOVE

Loving our neighbors—or our enemies, for that matter—has nothing at all to do with morals or ethics. Rather, Kabbalah teaches that love is a formidable weapon in furthering our own cause in life, which is simply to gain true joy and fulfillment. In other words, we benefit.

Love is a weapon of Light, and it has the power to eradicate all forms of darkness. That is the key. When we offer love even to our enemies, we destroy their darkness and hatred—which is the reason they became our enemies in the first place! What's more, we cast out the darkness inside ourselves. What's left are two souls who now recognize the spark of divinity they both share.

This Name also awakens love for our spouse, friends, family, and self. After all, we can share only what we possess. Thus, we cannot love our neighbor or our spouse if we don't possess a love for our own self. Use this Name to dissolve animosity and bitterness that might arise after an argument with loved ones.

MEDITATION

Like attracts like! By emulating the Creator's unconditional love for all humankind, you bring love into your own life. You create harmony between yourself and other people, and between humanity and the natural world.

# UNCONDITIONAL LOVE

*A student once approached a sage who was well-versed in the spiritual doctrines and mystical arts. He asked the master to teach him all the sublime secrets of life—to explain all the magnificent mysteries of the cosmos that are hidden in all the holy books. And he asked if all this could be done in the time that a person can remain balanced on one leg. The great sage carefully considered this request. He smiled warmly and replied: "Love thy neighbor as thyself. All the rest is commentary. Now go and learn."*

## HEAVEN ON EARTH

The concept of a *heaven on earth*, according to Kabbalah, refers to both individual and global peace. This same principle also holds true in regard to the concept of messiah. There is a personal messiah and a universal *messiah*.

But we must first achieve our own internal liberation and recovery through personal transformation. Namely, we must achieve a state of messiah within our self. Only when individual transformation in the world reaches critical mass, will universal peace, harmony, and a global messiah materialize before our very eyes. So, as seen through the lens of Kabbalah, the global messiah is not a savior but rather a seal and a sign that enough individuals have transformed their lives and, in turn, our world.

This is a constant and recurring theme in Kabbalah; everything, including our destiny of heaven on earth, begins and ends with our own individual behavior.

This Name quickens the process on every level.

## MEDITATION

You ignite the Light of the messiah within yourself, within others, and throughout the planet. The concept of heaven on earth becomes conceivable and achievable.

# HEAVEN ON EARTH

It may be hard to believe, but chaos and, yes, even death are temporary distractions of this physical world, necessary for the game of life. Our true purpose is to have unending happiness and eternal existence. We can create heaven on earth.

## FAREWELL TO ARMS

Conflict and war among nations begin with friction between individual people. A nation at war is simply the effect of spiritual darkness born of animosity and intolerance among individuals who comprise the nation. As long as brothers or friends can find reason to clash with one another, nations will devise reasons for bloody battle.

We've been duped into believing that our actions toward others have no impact upon the world at large. Wrong! Not only do interactions between two people contribute to the state of the world, each interaction totally and completely transforms the world! But it's difficult to detect this global makeover because everyone else's actions are *also* trans-forming the planet at every moment. The state of the world is merely the sum total of human interaction.

When enough people make the effort to find good in one another, nations will suddenly and miraculously discover ways to achieve a lasting harmony.

There it is—the long-hidden formula for world peace. It begins with us. Peace flourishes when we extend tolerance, unconditionally, to our neighbors. Be aware with complete conviction that our efforts are changing the *entire* world in that one moment.

## MEDITATION

Just as the light of a bulb banishes darkness from a room, conflict on every scale—between people arguing about a parking space, or between nations arguing about an oil field—is brought to a peaceful end through the Light of this Name.

# FAREWELL TO ARMS

Solutions for peace are never political, philosophical, or militaristic. Violence, even when justified, is merely fighting darkness with more darkness. Solutions must be founded upon spiritual Light and the human soul.

## LONG-RANGE VISION

Kabbalah teaches that ten "curtains" are implanted in our consciousness, limiting our ability to perceive the true reality. As a result, we fail to judge situations accurately. We may get ourselves involved in a relationship, confident that we've made the right decision, but it turns out to be the worst mistake of our life. Business opportunities that appear lucrative at the outset become financial black holes.

Likewise, situations that initially appear hopeless can be blessings in disguise.

Lacking the ability to see the long-term consequences of short-term decisions, we have a maddening tendency toward misjudgment.

Before entering into a marriage, a business partnership, or any new venture, we can utilize this Name to ascertain whether trouble awaits us ten to fifteen years down the road.

MEDITATION

You have the power of clear vision and foresight in every part of your life. The blindfolds are removed. You grasp the cause-and-effect relationship that governs all reality. Your life choices and actions are motivated by ultimate results, not momentary illusions. You see more through your eyes; you perceive more through your mind's eye; you feel more through your intuition.

# LONG-RANGE VISION

How many times have we thought, "I should have seen it coming"? Our lives are often full of heartache and problems simply because we failed to really "see" the situation confronting us. But suppose we could foresee all the consequences of the future *right now*...

## DUMPING DEPRESSION

Ascending the spiritual ladder requires far more greatness and strength than conquering nations, building empires, or attaining great wealth.

The negative forces (our ego) that dwell in the world use a two-step plan against us. They:

1. Make us fall
2. Keep us down through feelings of guilt and depression over our setbacks

Getting up again generates *greater* spiritual Light in the world than if we had never fallen in the first place. The fact that we fell is not what's important. True greatness lies in the act of rising again.

But depression is an alluring emotional state. In point of fact, it's downright tempting, for it, too, arouses energy within a downhearted individual. But the nature of this energy is negative and nocuous, whereas the spiritual energy of the Light is positive and transformational.

When we rise out of our depression with the intent to reveal Light in the world, positive energy envelops us, bringing great blessings and untold joy to all existence.

## MEDITATION

The emotional strength to stand after you stumble, to rise after you fall, and to endure when the path seems unendurable is bestowed upon you.

Life is fraught with obstacles and tests that sometimes knock us off our feet. When we do lose our balance and fall flat on our faces, it's important to stand up again rather than to sink into doubt and depression...

and dust ourselves off.

# DUMPING DEPRESSION

## GREAT ESCAPE

"Prison?" you ask.

Unquestionably.

*We're hostages to the constant pressure to outdo friends and colleagues. We're in bondage to our reactive whims and self-absorbed desires. We're captive to our jobs and financial pressures. We're prisoners to other people's perceptions of us. We're incarcerated by our need for other people's acceptance.*

Want to break out?

The ego is the foundation of all forms of misery. It compels us to convince others that we're right, even when we're wrong, and even when we *know* we're wrong. Ego gives us the illusion that we act freely, but in reality we are captive to its desires.

When a person denies that he or she has an ego, well, that is just the ego hard at work, doing its job, patrolling the prison grounds.

If an individual cannot recognize his or her own ego in a situation, the ego simply blinded the person by placing this individual into *solitary confinement.*

Ego is a ball and chain that anchors us to the physical dimension, and blocks our connection to spiritual growth—yet it is only in the spiritual realm that true joy and fulfillment can be found.

## MEDITATION

This Name brings the greatest of all freedoms: escape from ego-based desires, selfish inclinations, and the "me first" mentality. In their place, you gain life's true and lasting gifts—family, friendship, and fulfillment.

We're in prison and we don't even know it!

# GREAT ESCAPE

## FERTILITY

If we believe, erroneously, that we are the ultimate source of our abundance, blessings, and miracles, then our lives inevitably become as barren as a desert. Souls become sterile due to inflated self-importance.

Giving birth to children, giving birth to new ideas, or giving birth to a business solution all require the divine force of fertility. Fertile minds and fertile bodies bring forth the kinds of miracles and blessings that lead us to fulfillment in the deepest sense.

Acknowledging and appreciating this profound truth kick-starts this Name and launches it into action.

MEDITATION

Abundance and fruitfulness fill your being. You are imbued with the power of procreation. You can also meditate upon others who are trying to start a family.

# FERTILITY

Sometimes a couple finds it difficult to conceive a child. This Name is the *spiritual DNA of fertility*.

## DIALING GOD

The Light is always there, never changing, forever willing and able to fulfill our every desire, to answer our every prayer. Just like the electricity in our homes, it is ever present, but we must plug into it in order to physically receive its many benefits.

There are many negative forces that attempt to block and impede our prayers as they travel the spiritual network. We create these negative forces with our own negative behavior and unkind words. In the same way as freezing rain and ice can down a power line, our cold and bitter behavior breaks down the lines of communication to the source of all blessings.

This Name clears all obstructions, provided we acknowledge that we alone are responsible for getting our prayers answered. It repairs broken lines, removes interference, and establishes a secure line of communication to the Upper World.

## MEDITATION

You dial. You connect. Your prayers are answered at the speed of "Light."

# DIALING GOD

Are you constantly getting a busy signal when you
pray? Is there too much static on the line? Are you
constantly getting cut off each time you dial up?
Is it hard to get an outside line?

## VICTORY OVER ADDICTIONS

The selfish desires of our body were given complete dominance over the aspirations of our soul so that we could *earn* the Light of fulfillment through the challenges that accompany transformation. Consequently, it will always be easier to succumb to reactive, selfish impulses than to act with tolerance and kindness toward others—especially when infuriating people push our buttons all day long.

It takes no effort to blindly and mindlessly follow the whims of ego. But strength and endurance are needed to make the true longings of the soul victorious. However, it's a battle that cannot be won by humans alone. We need the assistance of the Light of the Creator if we are to reclaim control over our lives and liberate the power of our souls.

Victory is ours for the taking.

### MEDITATION

Recall any nasty habits or unpleasant character traits that you cannot get rid of. This Name ensures your victory over the forces of ego. You are imbued with the emotional power and discipline to triumph over all self-centered impulses and negative desires.

# VICTORY OVER ADDICTIONS

Did you notice that a bad habit is easier to develop than a good habit? It's easier to develop an addiction to chocolate than to steamed zucchini or daily exercise.

Want to make changes that last more than four weeks? You've come to the right Name!

## ERADICATE PLAGUE

*Today, 4,000 teens started smoking. In the next three minutes, a woman will be diagnosed with breast cancer. One-third of the world is now infected with tuberculosis. In the next twelve months, over 180,000 men will be afflicted with prostate cancer. Before finishing elementary school, the average American child will have seen 8,000 murders on TV. In the next 60 seconds, 12,000 tons of carbon dioxide will be pumped into the atmosphere. In the next 60 minutes, 1,800 children will die of malnutrition and hunger. By tomorrow, 25,000 people will die of water shortage or contamination. Over 25 million Americans purchase nicotine products. One in 1,500 college students is HIV positive. One out of every four females has an eating disorder. In the next twelve months approximately 13 million people will be victims of crime.*

Today, if a dozen people in a single location suddenly fall ill, the media declares an epidemic. But when more than 500,000 people die from smoking-related illnesses in a single year, no one calls it a plague!

There are two reasons for this: The deaths were spread over time and space. They occurred over the course of a year, and they took place in different parts of the world. The influence of time and space blinds us to the reality of the modern-day plagues that lurk among us.

This Name is both the antidote and the preventative medicine for the root cause of all plagues that can afflict our world.

MEDITATION

Think about smoking, cancer, AIDS, pollution, nuclear waste, depression, heart disease, hatred, or any other plague that infects the world. Now summon forth Light to wipe out these plagues at their root.

# ERADICATE PLAGUE

The Kabbalists tell us that the concept of plague has a wider meaning than the biblical hailstones, frogs, and darkness. The plagues that appear in our generation are far more subtle and deceptive. No need to feel paralyzed and hopeless—we can remove plagues at their seed.

## STOP FATAL ATTRACTION

Negative, destructive people too often find their way into our lives. At first they can be fun, friendly, and very cool to hang out with. We may believe they want to be close friends, or that they genuinely want to help us. But they end up stealing our energy and depriving us of our spiritual Light. The result? Our defenses are weakened and we become vulnerable physically, mentally, emotionally, and spiritually.

Two thousand years ago, the high priests in the holy temple of Jerusalem used this powerful Name to extinguish negative energy and to replenish the spiritual Light that was lost through contact with a negative or wicked person.

### MEDITATION

Here you become the high priest in the temple of your own being. Through the power of this Name, your soul is imbued with divine energy, and evil people are banished from your presence.

Did you ever wonder why you attract so many of the wrong people into your life?

Thought so.

STOP FATAL ATTRACTION

## SHARING THE FLAME

Darkness and evil are powerless in the presence of Light.

The relationship between light and darkness in the everyday world reveals a profound secret of spirituality. Darkness can exist *only* in the light's absence. Sharing the wisdom of these 72 Names with another soul is akin to lighting a candle in our darkened world, for the knowledge and the letters themselves are the stuff and substance of spiritual Light. The more we share these tools, the more we diminish our own selfish nature and the darkness throughout the world.

The letters of this Name are derived from a biblical verse on the Tree of Life, and its power is to bring immortality and endless joy. Kabbalah teaches that *Tree of Life* is a coded reference to the unseen Upper World, where 99 percent of reality resides. This infinite hidden dimension is the true source of all joy, wisdom, and enlightenment.

## MEDITATION

Concentrate on sharing Light with friends, family, and the entire family of humankind. Take this Name with you, out into the real world, and share these tools with others. Ask for the strength to walk the talk.

In your mind's eye, envisage openings and opportunities in the world for the global dissemination of this ancient wisdom.

Know that this Name is arousing the forces of immortality and increasing joy in the world. Expect and demand nothing less.

## SHARING THE FLAME

מלה

A single candle lessens the darkness of a large auditorium—but no amount of darkness can extinguish the flickering flame. Even if the darkness were expanded it would have no effect on the candle's radiance.

## JEALOUSY

The Upper World is like a vast cosmic echo chamber. Curse the heavens, and what happens? The echo chamber returns the curse to its point of origin!

Kabbalah tells us the elevated region of the Upper World is stirred when our own world stirs. The concepts of "above" and "below" refer both to the spiritual and physical aspects of human beings—the body and soul—and to the "upper" and "lower" stirrings of the cosmos and Earth.

Everything is tied together in a single, stirring dance of Creation.

The chaos and strife that afflicts our generation originates from negative forces swirling in the Upper Worlds. But these dark forces originate in the individual and collective actions of human beings. They echo our own destructive deeds.

Though we may find it difficult to accept, our hurtful words, jealous stares, and envious thoughts about others have a cumulative negative effect in the spiritual realm, which in turn generates personal and global suffering. To eradicate the darkness and chaos from human existence, we must extinguish the parallel forces in the Upper Worlds through the power of this Name.

## MEDITATION

You ascend into the Upper World to diminish the forces of darkness caused by your jealous stares and envious thoughts, in turn, you lessen the pain and suffering in the world.

When the problems of the world weigh heavy upon us—poverty, famine, disease, terror, and hatred—we can do something about it. Address the underlying root cause—our own jealousy.

רוחו

## JEALOUSY

## SPEAK YOUR MIND

It's difficult to be lovingly truthful with others. When an opportunity arises to confront someone with the truth, we lock up; our hearts race and our adrenaline pumps at the mere prospect of speaking our mind.

Fear of speaking or hearing the truth is the biggest stumbling block we face in our desire to experience genuinely fulfilling, honest, and loving relationships. When we hold something back, that *something* separates us from the other person. If we're not open to hearing the words of others without reacting or taking them personally, we have distanced ourselves from those individuals.

It's always easier to tell people what they want to hear. It's often more comfortable to agree with someone, even if we disagree in our hearts. And since it can be equally frightening to confront painful truths about our own selves, our friends and family may feel compelled to tell us only what we want to hear.

## MEDITATION

When you need to tell the truth, this Name brings you courage to open your heart as well as your mouth.

When you need to hear the truth, this Name brings you strength to open your ears and close your mouth.

# SPEAK YOUR MIND

*I never give them hell. I just tell them the truth and they think it's hell.*
   —Harry Truman

When you need to speak the truth but find it difficult, utilize this Name as soon as your heart starts beating rapidly. Likewise, when you need to be open to harsh truths about yourself, use this Name the minute your back gets up.

## ORDER FROM CHAOS

*Anything that can go wrong, will.*
    —Finagle's Law of Dynamic Negatives

*If there are two or more ways to do something, and one of those ways can result in a catastrophe, then someone will do it.*
    —Edward A. Murphy, Jr. (Murphy's Law)

*The chance of the bread falling with the buttered side down is directly proportional to the cost of the carpet.*
    —Jennings' Corollary to Murphy's Law of Selective Gravity

*The other line always moves faster.*
    —Etorre's Observation

*There's never time to do it right, but always time to do it over.*
    —Meskimen's Law

The numerical value of this particular Name is seven, a highly significant number in Kabbalah. There are, say the Kabbalists, ten dimensions that form reality. The highest of these ten dimensions, called the Upper Three, exist outside our physical reality. The Lower Seven, however, directly interact with our physical world. For this reason, the number seven turns up in many places: seven colors of the spectrum, seven notes of the musical scale, seven seas, seven major continents, seven days in a week, seventh day of rest.

Things can go dreadfully wrong in the world—and in our lives—when these seven dimensions are out of alignment!

## MEDITATION

Harmony always underlies chaos. With this Name, balance and serenity are restored among the seven days of the week. Order emerges from chaos. Not only will your toast not fall on the buttered side, it won't fall at all!

# ORDER FROM CHAOS

I had never had a piece of toast
Particularly long and wide
But fell upon the sanded floor
And always on the buttered side.
    —James Payn

## SILENT PARTNER

There are two kinds of wealth: spiritual and physical.

How these spiritual and material assets get divvied up depends upon which silent partner we choose; after all, every partner wants a piece of the action.

If we choose the Dark Force as our silent partner, it will allow us to keep 100 percent of our material wealth but it demands 90 percent of our spiritual Light, of which it then tithes 10 percent back to us in the form of momentary gratification. The Dark Force then uses the remaining 90 percent of the Light to strengthen itself and wreak havoc in the world (and in our personal lives).

If we choose the Light as our silent partner, we will keep 100 percent of the Light and 90 percent of the physical wealth. All we must do is tithe 10 percent back to the Light in the form of charity.

The concept of tithing, of giving away 10 percent of our earnings, is also designed to *remove* the Dark Force's influence from our lives.

If the negative force remains attached to our financial sustenance, eventually its influence will wither away our good fortune. Tithing 10 percent of our income does not diminish our well-being. On the contrary, it brings greater prosperity and joy in every area of our lives. The silent partner effect means that we always have one side or the other with us. The choice is ours.

## MEDITATION

Tithing—and meditation upon this sequence of letters—removes the Dark Force's presence from your earnings, and its destructive influence from your life. The Light is now your silent partner, bringing you endless blessings and protection. It's a partnership made in heaven!

# SILENT PARTNER

Everyone who comes into this world must choose a "silent partner"—the Dark Force or the Light of the Creator. Take your pick.

## SOUL MATE

When a single unified soul is set to enter into this material dimension, it is first divided into two halves—male and female. As these two halves of one soul undergo transformation in the physical world, either through suffering and ordeal or through proactive spiritual transformation, they progressively draw closer to one another. The uniting of two halves of one soul is an inevitable fate, but the timing depends upon their level of spirituality.

When the time is ripe, true soul mates find one another *even* if they are worlds apart— whether physically, on opposite sides of the globe, or spiritually, with contrasting lifestyles and backgrounds.

Moreover, the concept of soul mates does not refer only to marriage. The concept of soul mates also applies to relationships with friends, business colleagues, and partners in every sort of shared endeavor.

## MEDITATION

The energy of soul mates is aroused through this sequence of letters. You attract the other half of your soul. All of your existing relationships are deeply enriched, imbued with soul mate energy.

# SOUL MATE

Looking for the perfect date, the ideal mate, true
friends, loyal associates, or the right business partner?

## REMOVING HATRED

All destruction—including even natural disasters—occurs for one reason: humanity's hatred toward our fellow beings.

Kabbalah teaches that tornadoes, floods, earthquakes, and disease are born from the collective hatred that burns in our hearts. In truth, there is no such thing as a natural disaster, despite what our insurance policies say. Human behavior and the human heart are the sole determining factors as to what occurs in our environment and what transpires between nations.

Here's what the ancient Kabbalists had to say on this matter: *If a person witnesses any form of hatred—on his own street or anywhere in the world—it means this person still has some measure of hatred lingering in his own soul.*

If we harbor even the slightest bit of hatred or animosity for another person—for any reason whatsoever, valid or invalid, whether we're aware of it or whether we're in self-denial —we still bring destruction to the world.

By cleansing the hatred in our own hearts, we can remedy all the world's problems at once at the level of their root cause.

MEDITATION

Be painfully honest! Acknowledge every person or group of people toward whom you feel anger, envy, malice, total disgust, or any combination thereof. With the Light of this Name, drop those negative feelings like a load of wet laundry!

> *I have seen the enemy, and they are us.*
> —Pogo

# REMOVING HATRED

## BUILDING BRIDGES

This is one of the few Names that can be pronounced in English. It sounds like *Om*, or *Aum*. It is the origin of the *Om* mantra chanted in spiritual systems of the East.

A visual meditation upon these unique shapes generates the highest connection to the Upper World. It creates a bridge between physical reality and the ultimate source of joy and fulfillment in the spiritual dimension.

However, in building a bridge to the Upper World, we must also build bridges with the people in our lives—friends and foes included. We must first repair some of the relationships in our lives.

We cannot obtain one without the other.

### MEDITATION

With the power of this Name, you extend the hand of friendship to individuals with whom you're in conflict—even if they owe you money! You awaken compassion and summon the courage to pick up the phone and dial that person right now. And that means right now! Accordingly, a bridge to the Upper World will be erected on your behalf.

# BUILDING BRIDGES

When our prayers go unanswered—when there is more darkness than Light in our lives, when confusion reigns over order—there is one reason: We have severed our connection to the perfect realm of the Upper World.

## FINISH WHAT YOU START

Obstacles—both external and self-imposed—often stop us from achieving our objectives. It's easy to be excited and optimistic at the start of a new endeavor. Challenges of many kinds, however, often prevent us from reaching our goals. We procrastinate and we postpone—and our passion wanes.

Internal obstacles include fear, frustration, forgetfulness, doubt, and laziness.

External challenges come in all shapes and sizes, but they're only a test. The imposing proverbial brick wall is usually a soft and cushy curtain artistically painted and cleverly disguised to look like a brick wall—*just to keep us from even trying to pass through!*

No one said the road to personal achievement and spiritual greatness was an easy one. But it's a road that can be successfully walked and completed along a picturesque and scenic route.

## MEDITATION

You're endowed with the power to conclude everything you begin, especially tasks and goals of a spiritual nature.

Whenever you feel like quitting...

# FINISH WHAT YOU START

## MEMORIES

When we make a huge mistake in our lives, and we wind up paying for it dearly, we vow never to repeat it. We've learned our lesson, we tell ourselves. But as time goes by, the pain of our error gradually fades away and soon we forget the price we paid.

According to Kabbalah, the opportunity to repeat the same error inevitably returns to us, this time in a slightly dissimilar form, perhaps through a different circumstance or a different person. But the underlying problem is the same. We must confront this error over and over again until we internalize the lesson and remove the negative trait that led us to slip up in the first place.

Each time we repeat the same mistake, our pain and our payment increase.

## MEDITATION

The power of memory arises within your consciousness. Lessons of life are deeply ingrained into your being, including the lessons and wisdom filling the very pages of this book. This Name also removes negative memories and activates greater memory retention.

# MEMORIES

Do you constantly make the same mistake over and over again? Would you love to break the cycle?

## REVEALING THE DARK SIDE

Our purpose in life is to find the Light that was hidden at the moment of Creation. That purpose can be fulfilled only if we identify the actual hiding spot, which is *all* our negative traits, each and every last one of them.

We can come into this world blessed with a nature that's 99.9 percent positive. But there can still be one microscopic negative trait buried somewhere inside. If we ignore it, life gently knocks us on the head. If we still ignore it and wonder, "Why me?" the knock becomes harder.

So, what are good people like us supposed to do?

When sunlight shines through a set of window blinds, thousands of dust particles are visible in the shafts of light. But until the sunlight arrived, we couldn't detect the dirt and dust swirling in the air.

The Light of this Name works in the same way. When we allow this spiritual Light to shine in our lives, it reveals any self-centered qualities that still taint our nature.

Activate this Name when you find yourself asking, "What did I do?"

## MEDITATION

Light shines. You recognize the negative forces still active within yourself. Your reactive impulses are no longer a mystery. With the power of this Name, they're history!

> *The greatest trick the Devil ever played was convincing the world he didn't exist.*
> —Keyser Soze, *The Usual Suspects*

Did you ever wonder why seemingly bad things happen to good people?

# REVEALING THE DARK SIDE

## FORGET THYSELF

The Tree of Life refers to the Upper World that exists beyond our five senses—an endless dimension filled with Light and divine energy. The Tree of Life is a realm of utter perfection.

When we are healed from an illness, the Light of healing flows from this realm. When we are financially successful, the force of prosperity derives from this dimension. When a life is created, the life-force that sustains all living creatures issues from this idyllic reality.

But there's a caveat: The Tree of Life will extend a branch down into this world only if there is an intense desire to cling to its branches. Deep yearning summons forth the Tree of Life.

One thing stops us from doing so—ego.

We are our own worst enemies. We allow our egos to get in the way of our success. We cling to our own opinions. The more people oppose us, the more entrenched we become in our own ideas. It pains us terribly to let go of long-held views.

It's human nature to expend whatever energy is required to prove a point, no matter the cost. As a result, we're seduced into making decisions that gratify the ego but injure the common good. We often reject the ideas of others because they didn't originate in our own clever little minds. We may even secretly wish for failure—even if we ourselves are damaged by it—if a plan originates from someone who ignored our advice.

## MEDITATION

You are now transcending the limits of yourself so that you cling to the Tree of Life. Happiness finds you, now that the ego is out of the spotlight. You master the art of getting out of your own way, letting go of all stubbornness.

# FORGET THYSELF

We constantly get in our own way. We think we're smart, clever, and able to solve our problems on our own, without any help from above. This Name nudges us aside, allowing the Light to come in and do the job.

## SEXUAL ENERGY

We tend to view sex as a mechanical sport, instead of a sacred, soulful act that can deliver long-term lasting pleasure. In Kabbalah the cosmic and the erotic are intimately intertwined.

There is a clear-cut connection between the vast universe and our personal sex life. Attraction, arousal, touch, friction, sparks, and the fusion of two people in lovemaking all have enormous mystical implications. A lover's kiss or sensual caress contains sparks of the Light.

Each time a male and female unite in love, our physical world mates with the Upper World, bringing Light to all existence. Thus, lovemaking is also "Lightmaking" . . . for the couple locked in embrace and for the world at large. It's an experience that can only be described as *divine sex*.

The key to this unification is avoidance of selfish sex. Self-centered desire and ego prevent a cosmic connection, and that's when sexual energy begins to drain from our own relationships.

### MEDITATION

You purify your desires so that you share love and energy with your partner, putting his or her needs ahead of your own. You ignite sexual energy so that your passion helps elevate all existence. You replenish the Light that was lost due to any prior selfish sexual activities.

# SEXUAL ENERGY

Sex sizzles with intense energy and provokes heightened consciousness. But it's not enough to turn on; we must have courage to *tune in* also. By tuning in to the spiritual purpose of sex, we ignite passion in our sexual energy. This Name is our key to the ignition.

## FEAR(LESS)

Before we reach paradise and plentitude we must first journey through a barren desert. Before there is Light, there is darkness.

Our personal effort to create Light out of darkness expresses humanity's most profound longing and deepest desire: to be the actual cause of our own happiness. Make no mistake, it was the souls of humanity—you and I—who chose this path to transformation and fulfillment.

Our fears are often the greatest obstacles that confront us. They can burden and encumber our existence to the point where we are preoccupied simply with coping with them. Well, forget about coping. This Name is about curing!

Incapacitating fear is an illusion. Fear is a bluff, and we must call the bluff—because on the other side of fear lies paradise! If we run away from our fears, we are fleeing from the fulfillment of our own deepest longings and needs.

## MEDITATION

Ask yourself, "What am I afraid of?" The courage to conquer your fear now rises within you. By proactively confronting your fears at the seed level, you pull them out by the roots. You *extirpate* them (look it up!) entirely from your being.

# FEAR(LESS)

Life is not about *coping* with fears, it is not about *surviving* bouts of anxiety or just *working our way* through panic attacks. Life is about achieving absolute happiness, complete freedom, and true fulfillment.

Don't settle for less.

## THE BIG PICTURE

A small girl sees an apple seed for the first time. She is not sure what to make of it.
One day, she sees her father burying the seed in the ground. Then a tree grows, bearing
bright red, shiny apples. From now on, when the girl sees a seed, she also sees the
tree hidden within it.

One day the girl picks an apple from the tree—and within it she discovers a bunch of
apple seeds. *Now* when she looks at an apple seed, she perceives the tree, the apple,
the new seeds, and even the many future apple trees that will one day come into being.
All this is understood in one moment, simply by glancing at one seed.

This is how wisdom really works. It's easy to get stuck in the details of life and to miss the
big picture. We perform actions without any regard to their future consequences. But as
the apple is contained in the seed, every effect that materializes in our lives has its origin
in a prior action performed *by us.*

Seeing the big picture means learning to become the Creators of our own fulfillment:
to realize that the Light is the source of all joy, and to settle for nothing less! It means
grasping the purpose behind a problem and the potential Light that awaits us when we
proactively confront our problems.

## MEDITATION

This Name raises your awareness of the long-term effects of all your actions. You see
the big picture of the spiritual challenges in every moment before they can become
the foundations of chaos and crises.

# THE BIG PICTURE

When we want to grasp what life is really all about, these letters give us the "big picture," which always includes the blessings that are hidden in the obstacles and challenges that confront us.

## CIRCUITRY

Constant *desire to receive for the self alone* creates a bottomless pit, a black hole that eventually leaves us in darkness. The dark side of our nature tells us that we're doing others a favor when we share. Our ego makes us oblivious to the fact that we receive when we give to others.

We can greedily and selfishly grab for all that life offers, or we can appreciate what we receive and share a portion of it with others. *Receiving for the sake of sharing* creates a circuitry, a constant flow of good fortune in our lives.

The secret behind sharing is found inside the numerical value of this particular Name of God, which is 118—the exact same numerical value of the Hebrew word for "will take."

When we share, we are actually *taking* and receiving blessings in return. But if we share with a consciousness of "giving something up," or "doing someone a favor," the circuitry is broken. Like light trapped in a black hole, the blessings that should have been ours are unable to reach us.

## MEDITATION

This Name helps you to receive when you share and share when you receive. You see the opportunity that sharing gives and you are aware that when you receive with the right consciousness, you are also sharing. This is the circuitry of life. Connect to it and you move out of the black hole and into the LIght.

# CIRCUITRY

חעם

Dictionary Entry: **black hole**
Noun

1. A cosmological phenomenon with a gravitational field so strong that even light cannot escape from it.
2. Something resembling a black hole, as something that consumes a resource continually: a financial black hole.

### DIAMOND IN THE ROUGH

The moment we shift our consciousness and recognize the spiritual value concealed within our hardships, a sparkling new diamond is formed. What's more, the bigger our obstacles, the more sparkling the diamond we create!

Kabbalah teaches that this Name is the secret spiritual tool used by Moses to bring manna from heaven when the Israelites were starving in the desert. Manna could have any taste a person could wish for. With this sacred Name of God, *we* gain the power to change darkness into Light, and burdens into blessings. We have the ability to transform all our circumstances into sources of joy and fulfillment.

A word of caution: Our own consciousness directly influences our reality. Namely, if our head space is negative, if we are self-absorbed, or feeling victimized by a problem, a chunk of coal remains a chunk of coal. What's more, the diamonds we already possess will inevitably slip through our fingers, lost until we raise our consciousness.

### MEDITATION

Here you accomplish nothing less than the complete transformation of negative situations into positive opportunities and blessings. Manna rains down upon you. Life begins to taste like anything your soul desires or imagines.

Diamonds are the crystalline form of carbon. Pressure over millions of years transforms a chunk of coal into a precious jewel.

In the same way, all of life's problems can be transformed into sparkling opportunities. With this Name, it doesn't have to take millions of years!

# DIAMOND IN THE ROUGH

## SPEAKING THE RIGHT WORDS

Words have power. They ignite spiritual forces that influence the events and circum-stances of our lives. For instance, Kabbalah says slanderous gossip actually increases airborne diseases in our world. Defaming a person's character absolutely inflicts spiritual and physical harm against the intended victim and upon the person voicing the words.

However, because of free will, these truths are concealed from our rational minds by an innate, egotistic narrow-mindedness toward all things metaphysical. Thus, it's easy for us to disregard and dismiss the power and influence of a spoken word and, along with it, *responsibility!*

Our words either emerge from our ego or from the Light. When we allow the Light to talk on our behalf, our speech fills others with hope, blessings, love, and inspiration.

According to Kabbalah, we come into this world with a predetermined number of negative words that we're allowed to utter. When this allotment is used up, death overcomes us.

Imagine if we spoke only positive words of Light?

## MEDITATION

Silence your ego. Push the mute button. Now call upon the Light to speak on your behalf, on all occasions, so that your every word elevates your soul and all existence.

Did you ever say something you deeply regretted
—*and found yourself paying for it dearly many years
later?* Words can wound others, but they can also
imbue us with blessings and transform our very reality.

# SPEAKING THE RIGHT WORDS

## SELF-ESTEEM

When the souls of humanity were created, they inherited the DNA of their Creator. According to the sages, this *God gene* in our soul remains dormant until we activate it through the technology of Kabbalah. It then becomes unleashed in direct proportion to our personal transformation and ascension up the spiritual ladder.

Ultimately, we have the power within us to resolve all our troubles. You see, God does not really answer our prayers. We do.

As we grow, transform, elevate, and evolve spiritually by confronting our own chaos head-on—not fleeing it by escapism or pseudo-spirituality—our own spark of divinity and godliness glimmers with ever-increasing brilliance.

It is in us.

It always has been.

MEDITATION

With the divine energy of this sequence of letters, you are connected to the power of the ancient high priests of the temple in Jerusalem to heal and establish wellness in all areas of life.

# SELF-ESTEEM

Instead of surrendering our fate to rabbis, priests, medicine men, doctors, lawyers, or other consultants, the 72 Names—and this Name in particular—empower us to establish our own connection to the Light and thus to solve our own problems. This is the original self-help technology!

## REVEALING THE CONCEALED

Kabbalah teaches that concealment always precedes revelation:

- A seed is concealed in the ground in order to produce a tree.

- A baby is concealed in the womb before it is born into our world.

- A new invention is concealed in the inventor's mind before it appears in material form.

- Electrical energy must be concealed in a wire to express its power in our lives.

- A writer conceals ideas and principles inside metaphors and stories in order to reveal universal truths in the mind of the reader.

The genuine Light of the Creator and the ultimate truths of life are also first concealed before they're revealed. It's up to us to strive to uncover these truths, to restore the Light into the world so that pain and suffering, deceit and hatred are eternally abolished from the landscape of human existence.

### MEDITATION

You bring forth the powers of observation to see the truth . . . and the courage to handle it!

מיב

# REVEALING THE CONCEALED

The ego distorts reality so that we see only what it wants us to see. This Name ends our tunnel vision and stops our delusions so that we perceive truth in our daily circumstances and see things as they really are.

## DEFYING GRAVITY

Everyone fantasizes about having the power of *mind over matter.* But according to Kabbalah, we already possess it! And we use it every day without even realizing it.

Here's the problem: Ninety-nine percent of our thoughts and consciousness are controlled by ego. Thus our negative thinking influences physical reality in a detrimental way. All the troubles of the world—disease, earthquakes, famines, crime, the concealment of God's Light, the lack of belief in the reality of the human soul—it's all the result of our negative self-centered consciousness. We create this reality every moment. Pessimism, doubts, and cynicism become self-fulfilling prophecies. More ironic is the fact that our innate ability of mind over matter is hidden from us *only* because we don't believe it to be true.

If we allow ego desires to guide our existence, we're forever imprisoned and ruled by physical matter. There's only so far we can go, and it isn't very far at all. We need to see beyond illusions. We need to unmask the players in the masquerade.

If we allow the authentic yearnings of our souls to be our prime motivating force in life, as opposed to the illusory temptations of the material world, *mind over matter* will become our new reality.

How do we accomplish this?

By continually rejecting self-centered behavior, we gain the ability for mind to absolutely control the material world in a purely positive, constructive, and miraculous manner.

### MEDITATION

You unleash the power of mind over matter, the soul over the ego, and the spiritual over the physical. The goal is not to renounce the physical world but to eliminate its control over you and to become the true captain of your own fate. Everything becomes possible!

# DEFYING GRAVITY

Our true destiny is control of all reality through
the force of our imagination, with the power of our
thoughts guided by the Light within our souls.

How do we manifest this destiny?

## SWEETENING JUDGMENT

Though we're not aware of it, any negative behavior—even if it seems very minor—brings destructive forces into play. Whenever we speak in an uncivil or rude manner; whenever we cheat, lie, steal, insult, or harm other people—*Pop!*—we create a force of judgment. These negative forces are the unseen cause behind all the things that just "happen" to go wrong in our lives.

It may take minutes, months, or even years, but eventually we must confront the consequences of our reactive deeds.

Right now, obstacles are present in our lives because of the force called *judgment*—and judgments befall us to the degree that we inflict judgment upon other people. But Kabbalah teaches that our own words cannot serve as an indictment against ourselves. We cannot decree a judgment on our own being.

Life, therefore, is cleverly arranged so that we constantly meet and befriend people who commit errors and sins similar to our own. When we judge them, our own fate is sealed at that very moment.

But suppose we could refrain from judging friends, family, and undeserving foes. If this were possible, judgments against us could never come to pass.

MEDITATION

Through meditation upon this sequence, and with genuine penitence in your heart, you lessen or even revoke judgments set forth against you. And take an extra long moment to offer forbearance and compassion to others, so that these qualities of mercy are returned to you in equal measure.

Every word we speak, every action we perform is a boomerang flung into the cosmos. All these billions of boomerangs inevitably return to our lives—the positive ones and *all the negative ones*.

This Name helps us duck when negative boomerangs come hurling toward us.

לכה

# SWEETENING JUDGMENT

## THE POWER OF PROSPERITY

When you want to achieve real success—success without those nasty side effects—you must recognize that all good fortune originates from the Light of the Creator. If you believe that you're the sole architect of your success, the actual creator of your prosperity, you're worshipping ego and disregarding the power of the Light.

And that means you've been drawing your financial sustenance from the reactive system of human nature. You've been giving ego complete control of your life. Ego does have the power to bring financial gain and material pleasure, but at great cost to the buyer!

Each time you acquire an asset valued and prized by your ego, you trade away an asset treasured and cherished by your soul.

These are the only real business transactions that matter in life.

With this Name you draw good fortune from the Light, through your soul—not through your ego.

### MEDITATION

Acknowledge that the Light of the Creator is the ultimate source of all prosperity and well-being. Now summon the forces of prosperity and sustenance and ask for the strength to keep your ego in check when the other checks start rolling in.

# THE POWER OF PROSPERITY

If fortunes are continually won and lost in your life;
if you find yourself on a financial roller coaster;
if wealth has been gained at the expense of loving
relationships or good health; or if you're just plain
broke or short of cash...

## ABSOLUTE CERTAINTY

*Dictionary Entry:* **uncertainty principle**
Noun

1. *A principle in quantum mechanics holding that increasing the accuracy of measurement of one observable quantity increases the uncertainty with which other quantities may be known. Developed by theoretical physicist Werner Heisenberg in 1927.*
2. *Part of the present scientific view of the nature of physical reality, with implications for philosophy in general.*

If we inject doubt into any aspect of these teachings, we literally pull the plug and shut them down.

"I'll believe it when I see it" must be replaced by "I'll see it, when I believe it!"

And remember, certainty is not just confidence that we'll get what we want. Certainty means recognizing that we are *already getting* what we need for spiritual growth.

It's true that when hardship strikes, doubts begin to surface in our minds. We become uncertain about the reality of the Creator. We question the justice in the universe. We fear for the future. We point the finger of blame at others, or toward the heavens. But when we invoke the power of certainty, all these negative sensations fade away like fog shrouding a steadfast mountain.

In every area of life, the duration of chaos and pain is *always* directly proportional to our own degree of uncertainty and lack of responsibility.

## MEDITATION

Certainty! Certitude! Conviction! Sureness! Trust! All these fill your heart through meditation upon this Name.

# ABSOLUTE CERTAINTY

There's only one way to render all tools and power in this book inoperative and worthless. It is called *uncertainty*.

## GLOBAL TRANSFORMATION

World peace begins within the individual. Before we can change the human condition, we must change ourselves. It is often easy to rally around a cause. It is far more difficult to look in the mirror and begin the work of inner transformation.

If a beggar is in need of five dollars and a passerby has only a nickel, he cannot fulfill the beggar's needs. In other words, we can share only what we possess. Before we can embark on a mission to change the world, we must first transform ourselves, change our ways, and attain true joy and fulfillment in our own lives.

And if there is any doubt whatsoever that we ourselves still require further correcting, bear in mind the harsh Kabbalistic truth: That which our eyes witness out in the external world, all the evil, all the wickedness, is but a mirror image reflecting the remains of evil that lay hidden and undetected in our hearts.

MEDITATION

Reflect upon the spiritual truth that world peace begins with peace in your own heart. With this Name, you speed your own transformation—and strengthen the forces of peace throughout the world.

*You say you want a revolution, well, you know, we all want to change the world.*
    —John Lennon & Paul McCartney

# GLOBAL TRANSFORMATION

one world

## UNITY

Two people can have opposite opinions and conflicting viewpoints, yet both can be right. Enmity and bitterness occur when people respond *reactively* to one another, with intolerance to each other's view.

True spirituality disregards vague concepts of right and wrong. It aspires to a higher truth: the notion of unity, sensitivity, and tolerance for other viewpoints.

What good is being right if suffering and pain are the cost? What is so terrible about being wrong if personal peace, joy, and contentment are the rewards?

It is only the ego that worries itself with being right or wrong.

The soul's sole concern is unity, for unity begets peace and happiness.

When we treat others' viewpoints with dignity—especially when it's painfully difficult to do so—we often discover a new idea that brings blessings into our own life. This sacred Name should be used when we are stuck in our ways, clinging to our own long-held opinions and seething with anger and frustration at the ideas and beliefs of others.

## MEDITATION

Through these letters, you pass the true test of spiritual character: You're able to see all sides of the problems that come before you. Your focus is upon unity and soul as opposed to division and oneself.

Instead of trying to be right, we must recognize that there is a higher truth: unity! We need to seek harmony with our opponents—not because this is moral behavior, but because unity brings *us* lasting spiritual Light. It serves our own best interests.

מילה

## UNITY

## HAPPINESS

Too often we confuse temporary pleasure with enduring happiness because the trappings of the physical world are highly seductive and potent. When we are able to distinguish between the two, we will find true happiness. Pleasure is usually associated with egocentric desires, whereas happiness is linked to the longings of the soul.

By and large, our desires emerge from the selfish side of our nature. What we covet is not necessarily what will bring us lasting fulfillment. Happiness eludes us when we chase after what we want, as opposed to what we need. Our desires and cravings generally bring misfortune and turmoil after the initial pleasures and immediate gratifications have worn off.

We find true happiness when our lives are spent transcending our ego-based impulses to steadfastly pursue what our souls need for transformation and elevation.

In other words, when we're busy doing what we came to this earth to do in terms of spiritual work, we will meet deep-seated fulfillment every step of the way.

## MEDITATION

You find the strength to restrain selfish longings. Through this Name you are asking for what your soul needs, not what your ego wants. You find deep appreciation for whatever life brings you. This brings you happiness in the deepest sense.

# HAPPINESS

There is an old saying: Be careful what you wish for!

## ENOUGH IS NEVER ENOUGH

Two realities exist: darkness or Light. We can be in one or the other. But we tend to loiter in the gray areas. When we do achieve a little Light in our lives, we tend to excuse the little bit of darkness that we're still indulging.

But we came here to have it all! The goal is to banish *all* darkness and bask in absolute Light.

Sure, we'd like to believe that we are big thinkers. But in truth, we think small. It doesn't matter if there are billions of dollars in our bank accounts, or if we're running a Fortune 500 company, or running an entire country, for that matter.

Thinking big means to seek it all—*permanent happiness, spiritual greatness, eternal joy, our true soul mate, immortality, and peace on earth forevermore*—and to let go of every-thing else that prevents us from reaching that promised land.

Fifty billion dollars pales in comparison to never-ending fulfillment and a joy-filled eternal existence.

If we don't genuinely believe that these are attainable goals and our destiny, then we can't ever tell anyone that we know how to think big. Because the ego, the dark side of human nature, just duped us into thinking small.

Everything is possible. When we believe it, we will see it.

MEDITATION

Your eyes and heart remain focused on the end goal at all times. You awaken the persistence and passion to never—and that means *never*—ever settle for less!

# ENOUGH IS NEVER ENOUGH

We compromise in life. We settle for less. We sell out as soon we experience some enjoyment, and we wind up selling ourselves short!

This Name is about seizing the whole enchilada!

## NO GUILT

The concept of repentance is vastly misunderstood. It has nothing to do with a guilt trip. Or fear. Repentance is about repairing prior misdeeds by feeling the pain that we've caused to others and by abolishing the actual negative trait responsible for their hurt.

Through the power of repentance our souls journey back to the precise moment prior to our spiritual infraction. The damage is then undone, provided we have meditated with deep remorse to eradicate the character trait that originally induced our offense.

So how does this alleviate the suffering of the victim of our crime?

Kabbalah says there are no victims. The person who was injured by our misdeed warranted this negative act as a result of a misdeed that he or she committed at a prior time.

Our own pain and repentance are not the result of hurting an innocent victim. Rather, our remorse pertains to our being chosen as the "executioner" of the sentence, the deliverer of a judgment that was already decreed against this person.

And the pain we agree to take on is used to cleanse the nasty trait that led us to be a courier for wrongdoing in the first place.

A person who is spiritually pure and righteous will never be selected to execute judgment against a fellow human being.

## MEDITATION

Recall any negative deeds from your past. Reflect on some of your more unpleasant traits. Feel the pain of the people you have hurt. Ask the Light to eradicate all your negative attributes. The force called *repentance* spiritually repairs your past sins and diminishes the dark side of your nature.

# NO GUILT

Repentance purifies. It cancels judgments and it annuls sentences of death decreed against us in the Upper World.

## PASSION

A story is told of an old man who could neither read nor write. He desperately wanted to offer a prayer of gratitude to the Creator from a sacred prayer book, but he was unable to read the words on the page. However, his desire to connect to his Creator was great, so he began reciting the alphabet. He begged the Creator to assemble the letters into their proper sequences, to form the words of prayers.

A strictly religious passerby heard the old man reciting the alphabet. He laughed at the silliness of the man's prayer, and at that moment the gates of heaven were forever closed to the prayers of the religious man. In fact, the angels danced with joy as the old man's simple, sincere prayer ascended to the Upper World. The old man had illuminated heaven with the yearnings of his heart.

### MEDITATION

This Name stokes the fires of passion in your heart and in your soul. These letters give you the power to maintain sincerity, devotion, and correct consciousness in your prayers, your meditations, and your spiritual connections.

## PASSION

To truly ignite the power of prayer, we first need a fire burning in our own hearts.

## NO AGENDA

If you answered "yes" to the preceding questions, chances are your positive actions were contingent upon you receiving some form of benefit down the road.

We frequently befriend others or perform favors with a hidden agenda. The friendship we offer is usually conditional, without us even realizing it. We want something in return. It might be social standing. A loan. Or a favor that we would like to call in at some point in the future.

Our actions of sharing usually have strings attached as well. For instance, a patron's name is inscribed onto a plaque and then hung up in a lobby. A dinner is given in the benefactor's honor. A hospital wing is named after the charitable contributor. In Kabbalah, this is not considered unconditional sharing. True sharing is nameless so that the giver and the receiver have no idea who each other are. The giver gives. Period. Givers derive their pleasure from the unconditional anonymous act of pure sharing, expecting nothing in return. And that is when they receive everything!

When we give unconditional love and perform genuine actions of sharing, joy comes from our giving—not from what we want in return.

MEDITATION

Self-interest, ulterior motives, and hidden agendas give way to pure acts of friendship, unconditional love, and giving. In return, true and loving friends, joy, and fulfillment are attracted into your life.

# NO AGENDA

Do you ever feel let down by the people whom you befriended? Are you frequently disappointed by circumstances in which you gave so much of yourself?

If your answer to both questions is "no," skip this Name.

## THE DEATH OF DEATH

Make no mistake: The one and only angel of death is the cause whenever good things of any kind come to an end. By attacking death at the most fundamental level, we avert many of the fatalities that strike us. These letters are powerful weapons for making that attack!

With each set of eyes that falls upon this Name, the power of the angel of death is weakened throughout the world—until, ultimately, the "death of death" takes place and immortality reigns.

## MEDITATION

Meditate with total conviction and certainty upon the absolute demise of the angel of death, once and for all!

The power of death is not limited to the physical body. The end of a friendship, the failure of a business, the dissolution of a marriage are all expressions of death. When good things are in danger of coming to an end, this Name banishes death!

# THE DEATH OF DEATH

## THOUGHT INTO ACTION

Our dreams and aspirations are rooted in the purity of the Upper World. But our actions take place here in the material dimension, where a seemingly infinite variety of impediments can get in our way—everything from doubts and fears to mortgage payments and credit card debts. We are often inspired by brilliant thoughts, innovative ideas, and lofty goals. But we need to follow through and "close the deal." If this doesn't happen —if our intentions fail to manifest—it's a clear sign that we've lost our connection to the Upper World.

## MEDITATION

You are now reconnecting and reuniting the Upper and Lower Worlds through the power of this Name. By bringing these realms together, you find courage and commitment to accomplish your goals and achieve your dreams. Your thoughts become actualized. Your best ideas are transformed into action, and then into concrete results!

Typically, because of our own inaction, worthy goals and daring dreams never materialize. We procrastinate. We lose our passion. Or we simply give up. Our best ideas remain unrealized hopes. Our thoughts never become actualized.

Kabbalah has an explanation for this.

## THOUGHT INTO ACTION

## DISPELLING ANGER

To some degree, everyone is vulnerable to idol worship, whether through the pursuit of fame or the veneration of wealth and power. We revere images, especially the self-image we feel we must project to others.

The most blatant form of idolatry, according to Kabbalah, is anger. Something external is controlling our emotions and reactions.

When a computer crashes, losing our important files, and we erupt in anger, we have just bowed down before a silicon idol. When a car cuts us off on the freeway and we curse with rage, we are idolizing a metallic god. When we lose our temper with our spouse or children and cause them undue pain, we are worshipping an idol of darkness.

When we devote ourselves to idols, allowing external situations or other people to instigate anger and rage within us, we sever our connection to the Light. This is a big mistake, since the Light is the true source for the fulfillment of our deepest desires.

MEDITATION

You remove the power and allure of the world's controlling "idols" by invoking the power of this Name. Anger is purged from your heart. Your happiness and peace of mind are generated from within.

# DISPELLING ANGER

You may doubt that you've ever been an idol-worshipper —but *idol* refers to more than statues of lions or bulls. An idol is an object, person, or situation that dominates your behavior. Anger is a sign that you are in an idol-worshipping mode!

## LISTENING TO YOUR SOUL

Prior to Creation, all the souls of humanity were bound up as one unified soul. This soul shattered into countless sparks, bringing into being all the individual souls who were destined to walk this earth. That includes each one of us.

Each spark of soul must achieve its own individual transformation and spiritual purpose before the blessed unity of the one soul can be restored.

In business, in our relationships, and in our own personal connection to the Creator, there are clear-cut spiritual objectives that must be accomplished in order to bring peace and happiness to us and to the world.

But the world has failed to find its spiritual way and ultimate destination because the clamoring of the ego drowns out the calling of our soul. Ego constantly gives us the wrong directions, the incorrect instructions. We wind up in dangerous neighborhoods and dead ends in our pursuit of meaningless ambitions and empty materialistic goals.

## MEDITATION

The whispers of your soul and the divine counsel of the Light are heard loud and clear. You know what you have to do. You are willing and prepared to do what it takes to get it done.

Every one of us has a personal mission, a spiritual goal that we must achieve in this lifetime. But the interferences of the material world constantly derail us.

If we listen really carefully, our souls will direct us to our purpose, where we need to be.

# LISTENING TO YOUR SOUL

## LETTING GO

Our nature is to hang onto our pain and suffering. Our first inclination when happiness or the hope of a miracle stands before us is to say, "It's too good to be true."

This kind of consciousness is what prevents miracles and a joy-filled future from materializing in our lives.

We cannot have a fulfilling and miraculous future if we're hanging onto an unhappy and cynical past.

Nothing more need be said.

## MEDITATION

You let go. Of everything. Period.

# LETTING GO

It's often hard to let go of yesterday. We become prisoners to our past. We can't move forward. We can't get beyond past regrets and earlier traumas.

Here we receive the courage to let go!

Ready…Jump!

## UMBILICAL CORD

Whenever we commit a negative action, the Light instantly leaves our presence. We're floundering in the dark. We may not detect this effect with our five senses, but we experience it internally and through the events in our lives.

Our consciousness turns negative, our state of mind becomes gloomy and pessimistic. Situations around us spiral into darkness. We know we need to leave this space, fast, but we see no way out. We're alone, trapped, at the bottom of a snake pit. And the snakes are closing in quickly.

The good news is that there's a tool that can prevent us from completely severing the life-giving cord that connects us to the Light. This divine Name is the tool.

MEDITATION

You establish an umbilical cord to the divine energy, ensuring a constant glimmer of Light in your life, especially for those times when you wind up in a place of utter darkness.

# UMBILICAL CORD

When we experience moments of sadness, fits of anger, bouts of depression, or when we commit acts of intolerance or insensitivity, the divine radiance instantly withdraws, leaving us in spiritual darkness.

Unfortunately, in the chaos of day-to-day life, the "laundry list" above is bound to occur.

## FREEDOM

As slaves and the children of slaves, the people of Israel were in bondage in Egypt for 400 years. Then came Moses. Sent by the Creator, he won freedom for his people. Then he led them on a long and arduous journey, including that famous passage through the Red Sea. Eventually they reached Mount Sinai, where they had a date with destiny.

Strangely, however, the Israelites began complaining as soon as they escaped from bondage. They even begged Moses to lead them back into Egypt! How could this be possible? Was the journey through the desert worse than 400 years of slavery?

Kabbalah offers a startling explanation for this. The entire story is a code! It is a veiled narrative of individual spiritual transformation!

Let's decipher the code. *Egypt* refers to the human ego, the oldest slave master in history. Any aspect of our nature that controls us is *Egypt*. Egypt also denotes the seductive trappings of the material world.

The moment our spiritual path becomes challenging or uncomfortable for the ego, we long to return to our own personal Egypt—that is, to the lower level of being that we'd grown used to.

The path to transformation requires self-knowledge and personal accountability. It's not easy. We're constantly tempted to turn back. Escaping from spiritual bondage means liberation from the enslavement of our own former selves.

## MEDITATION

You perceive the balance and harmony that fills all Creation, especially in the hardships, challenges, and tests that you must face throughout life. With the power of this Name, you arouse strength to pass all those tests, to rise to a higher level of being, and to gain the joy and fulfillment that accompany true spiritual transformation. You unlock the chains of ego and achieve freedom!

As we begin to transform our lives and experience true fulfillment, we are tested again and again. Each test of our ego injects doubt. The optimism and excitement we felt at the start of our journey vanishes, we start to complain, the ego is back!

# FREEDOM

## WATER

According to science, water is the most mysterious and least understood substance in the universe. According to Kabbalah, water is the Light of God made manifest in the physical world.

Hence, water pollution is both a physical and spiritual crisis.

When the water in our lakes and the water in our cells are tainted with physical and spiritual toxins, our personal and global immune systems are dangerously weakened.

Genuinely pure water has the power to cleanse both physically and spiritually. In the same way that water miraculously dissolves dirt, grime, and filth from the physical body, water's metaphysical essence dissolves away the spiritual uncleanliness and negativity that we've brought upon our body and soul.

The Kabbalists say water can naturally heal, water can rejuvenate, and water holds the secret to immortality. But centuries of war, persecution, and hatred took its toll; thus water lost this intrinsic power.

This Name helps to return all water to its original divine and pristine state.

### MEDITATION

You purify the waters of earth, and awaken the forces of healing and immortality!

# WATER

The worst polluted body of water on the planet is not some highly contaminated lake. It is the human body, which consists of over 65 percent water.

## PARENT—TEACHER, NOT PREACHER

When we share the teachings and tools of Kabbalah with our children, amazing Light is revealed in our own lives, in the lives of our family, and throughout the world.

Although we participate in bringing our children into the world, we should remember that they are not ours, but are gifts given to us by the Creator in order to give us a chance to share, grow, and become kinder, more tolerant people. Our children give us an opportunity to be the Light and to spread the Light. In short, we need to become wise teachers, not loud preachers!

Instead of trying to preach the truth, or legislate wisdom, enlightened people know they must live the truth. A person who has been touched by the Light innately knows that he or she must become the embodiment of its power.

Therefore, like candles, we should allow the radiance of our thoughts and deeds to warm and enlighten our children. In this way, the changes in our own lives become examples and inspirations for them to follow.

MEDITATION

Desire to lovingly, respectfully, and selflessly share this wisdom with your children! The preacher in you is silenced. The teacher in you shines through in all your actions.

The greatest act we can perform in the physical world is helping another human being discover the radiance of the Light. That is the true purpose of being a parent.

# PARENT—TEACHER, NOT PREACHER

## APPRECIATION

Here's a simple question: Do you have a desire not to have an excruciating toothache?
Of course you do. Who in their right mind wants to experience a throbbing toothache?
But a moment before this question was posed, were you at all aware of this desire?
Of course not! And do you know why? It's because your desire *not to have a toothache*
was completely fulfilled. Namely, you didn't have a toothache so there was no need
to be aware of your innate desire not to have one. If, on the other hand, you had an
abscessed molar that was causing you much agony, you'd quickly become aware of
your desire not to want to have a toothache.

We have so many blessings in our lives that fulfill our existence. But we're not aware of
these spiritual treasures because our *fulfillment* leads us to complacency. We take important things for granted. Consequently, we must lose something in order to awaken our
desire for it. Remember, the Light wants to give us everything but we must have a desire
for it.

When we experience the pain of losing something dear to our hearts, a desire is awakened within us. But there is a far better way to activate all our desires for Light without
having to lose something. It is called *appreciation*.

When we truly appreciate everything, we feel like we have it all. And that's when we are
allowed to really have it all!

## MEDITATION

Appreciation. Thankfulness. Gratitude. These noble attributes are aroused by this
Name. Infused with these attributes, you retain and enjoy all the blessings and
treasures in your life.

# APPRECIATION

Do you find that you appreciate things only after they're gone? Do you look back over parts of your life wishing you had valued and cherished the things that are no longer there?

## CASTING YOURSELF IN A FAVORABLE LIGHT

Revealing our negative side attracts the evil eye. We become a magnet for the scorn of people around us. We invite their judgment into our lives—and all that destructive energy quickly begins to wreak havoc!

When we give people reason to focus on our good side, we avoid their negative influences and all the harmful side effects they can bring.

Moreover, as we make the effort to look beyond the imperfections of others, we magnify the power of this Name tenfold.

## MEDITATION

Your own being is lit beautifully, suffused with the Creator's radiance so everyone around you sees the positive, beautiful aspects of your self, as opposed to the distorted and dark image projected by the ego.

# CASTING YOURSELF IN A FAVORABLE LIGHT

מזל

With all of our mischievous misdeeds and rotten character traits, it's in our best interests when others see only the good side of our soul. In the language of filmmaking, this meditation is the ultimate "Lighting effect."

## FEAR OF GOD

*Fear of God* refers to an inner understanding of how our universe is "wired." Mistreating another person, for example, is like sticking our finger into a light socket. It's a cause that brings about a definite and painful effect—but it's not the electrical energy that needs to be feared, it's the *act* that brings us into dangerous contact with it.

*Fear of God* means seeing the future consequences of our present actions. For instance, if we could foresee the negative consequences attached to disrespectful behavior, our long-term vision would cause us to refrain. Our decision will *not* be motivated by morality or religious fear. It will be based on something far more persuasive: our own self-interest.

That power of acute observation comes to us through this Name.

MEDITATION

Awareness of the divine spark in every person is awakened in your heart. You become wiser in the ways of the world. You perceive the repercussions attached to your every word and deed, and you know that sharing acts toward others are always in your own best interest.

Fear of God does not refer to the religious notion of a Creator who punishes and rewards. The Light of the Creator is a thoroughly positive force, an endless spiritual energy whose only attributes are infinite sharing and love.

דחב

# FEAR OF GOD

## ACCOUNTABILITY

At one time or another, we all have asked ourselves (or God) this question. Life often hurts us, granted, but we have two options: hold onto our pain and wallow in self-pity, or accelerate our healing process and quickly climb to a new level of fulfillment and understanding.

Most of us consider ourselves *victims* when others do us wrong or when circumstances suddenly become chaotic. But any wrong done to us and any turmoil confronting us results from a negative action we committed in some area of our lives. The injury is merely the judgment—the effect of a cause that we ourselves initiated. Yes, this is a tough one to admit and accept.

If we let ourselves become consumed with feelings of revenge or victimization, we miss an opportunity to stop our reactive behavior, to rise above our problems, and to regain control over our lives.

When we accept judgment, on the other hand, it passes quickly. When we let go of self-pity and the dreaded "I'm the victim" syndrome, we let go of our pain at that same instant.

## MEDITATION

With these letters, impulses toward self-pity, retaliation, and revenge are swept away. You see that a "victim's mentality" is the foundation of all those feelings, and you replace that mentality with the understanding that you are the creator of your own circumstances. And you know that what you have created, you can change. Thus, everything changes now!

"Why me? Why now? What did I do to deserve this?"

# ACCOUNTABILITY

## GREAT EXPECTATIONS

Why do our most positive actions often go unrewarded for long periods of time? Kabbalah teaches that this is to allow a space for our free will to shine forth. Within this space, "great expectations" creep in to challenge us. "Tests of faith" confront us. We expect a quick return on our spiritual investments—but when time delays it, we become doubtful, deeply disappointed, hopeless, and helpless.

But we have *free will* to rise above these clouds of gloom and doom. By exercising this free will, we can truly earn our good fortune. Sometimes, of course, this can be an extremely difficult task. A great expectation is a formidable adversary.

The key to fulfillment is to simply shift our concentration away from results and expectations. Instead, we focus upon resisting our own impulsive reactions, which are nothing more than robotic responses to a given situation. In the moment that we resist expectation, we have exercised the sacred trait of free will.

The ego is no longer in control. We are. And that opens wide the door to all possibilities.

## MEDITATION

By meditating on this Name, you gain control over the power of time in your life. Instead of constantly demanding more of tomorrow, you appreciate what you have —and what you are—right now. False and self-seeking expectations are cast out!

# GREAT EXPECTATIONS

When you expect the world from your friends, your family, or from life, and they don't deliver, call upon this Name for some answers!

## CONTACTING DEPARTED SOULS

The human soul continues to rise to higher levels of existence after it leaves this plane of existence. This ascension can sometimes be difficult if a soul has accumulated undesirable baggage as the result of reactive behavior during his or her lifetime.

Through this Name we help elevate the souls of our loved ones in a pleasing and pleasant manner. We also receive counsel and messages from those whose love for us still radiates in the Upper Worlds.

### MEDITATION

Evoke the memories of loved ones who have passed on. Surround them with the Light of this Name. Meditate to elevate their souls to ever higher levels in the spiritual worlds. Open yourself up to receive their guidance and support.

# CONTACTING DEPARTED SOULS

Death is a sham. The souls of our departed loved ones continue to live on in a reality far more authentic than our illusory world. Through this Name, we make contact with the souls of family and friends who've passed on.

## LOST AND FOUND

There are times when we find ourselves off course in the journey of life. We feel lost. Bewildered. Confused. Life becomes an endless labyrinth, and we don't know which way to turn.

## MEDITATION

With this Name as your compass, the path toward your spiritual home is illuminated. You regain your bearings. With every step you take and with each moment that passes, you feel comfort, confidence, and a stronger sense of direction.

# LOST AND FOUND

When you want to find your way back home...

## RECOGNIZING DESIGN BENEATH DISORDER

Not a single blade of grass grows without direction from a higher power. Like an immense computer, the Creator's Light processes, calculates, and accounts for *everything* through the law of cause and effect.

When we react negatively to the apparently sudden chaos of life, we deny the underlying design and purpose of Creation. Our attitude prolongs the madness. But the moment we recognize and accept hardships and all chaotic circumstances as opportunities for spiritual elevation, pain and doubt quickly disappear. We alone determine the rate at which our turmoil and pain pass.

Be aware: The ego will constantly attempt to slow this whole process down to a sluggish crawl by concealing the order and the cause of the chaos in front of our eyes.

## MEDITATION

When you find yourself overcome with feelings of doubt or panic or with thoughts of doom, these letters reveal the order that underlies chaos. You become enlightened to the Creator's master plan as it pertains to your purpose in this world and to the problems you face.

There are no coincidences in life. No chance encoun-
ters. No random surprises. Whatever happens, happens
for a reason. So when our world feels out of whack
and we just want to scream, this Name is our fast track
to structure and serenity.

# RECOGNIZING DESIGN BENEATH DISORDER

## PROPHECY AND PARALLEL UNIVERSES

There are countless futures, all of which exist at the same time. That's right, ancient Kabbalists and contemporary physicists agree, parallel universes are a reality!

According to physics, the moment we make a decision, the universe splits and our alternative decision and fate branch out into another reality.

According to Kabbalah, parallel universes grow progressively more orderly, eventually reaching a world of paradise, happiness, and unending life.

However, our own behavior determines which universe we enter. Ego-driven actions keep us imprisoned in a universe of chaos. But the moment we resist our reactive responses, we make a quantum jump into an entirely different reality. Each new universe features a more fulfilled version of our lives. By recognizing opportunities to end reactive, egocentric behavior, we literally move from one world into another.

Prophecy is the ability to spot these opportunities. Prophecy is seeing the future in our present actions—seeing the consequences of reactivity versus the vast rewards that proactive behavior brings.

MEDITATION

The power of prophecy is bestowed upon you. With your consciousness elevated and your awareness heightened, you have the power to enter a new universe of transformation and Light.

# PROPHECY AND PARALLEL UNIVERSES

A prophet is not someone who sees into a predestined future. Indeed, there is no predestined future, because we have the ability to *re-create* the future at every moment. Therein lies the purpose of this Name.

## SPIRITUAL CLEANSING

Sometimes we lack the emotional courage and spiritual strength to correct all of our flaws.

What's more, our egos use many devious tactics against our own best interests. One of the most potent of these tactics is cynicism: the sense that anything but chaos should not even be *thought about* by an intelligent human being. This is a convenient escape from doing the hard work of spiritual transformation. It allows us to see ourselves as eternally blameless victims, rather than as responsible beings who are thoroughly accountable for the state of our own lives.

There are two ways to cleanse in life: pain or proactive spiritual transformation.

The path of pain hurts the body—our health, our finances, our personal lives. When we experience sickness or poor health, if we lose a business or go broke, if a marriage breaks up, or if there is heartache from children, this is all considered spiritual cleansing.

The path of proactive spiritual transformation only hurts the ego.

This Name focuses upon the ego, thus allowing us to purify and repair past iniquities in a merciful manner.

## MEDITATION

By meditating on these letters, you push REWIND and ERASE on your spiritual video. You are purified in your present life by correcting your transgressions from your lives in the past. This Name also cleanses our physical environment from spiritual impurities.

We all come into this world with spiritual defects that need correcting. These imperfections have accrued over previous lifetimes, and we cannot rid ourselves of their negative influences until they are mended.

בירם

# SPIRITUAL CLEANSING

72 NAMES CHART

| | | | | | | | |
|---|---|---|---|---|---|---|---|
| כהת | אכא | ללה | מהש | עלם | סיט | ילי | והו |
| הקם | הרי | מבה | יזל | ההע | לאו | אלד | הזי |
| וזהו | מלה | ייי | נלך | פהל | לוו | כלי | לאו |
| ושר | לכב | אום | ריי | שאה | ירת | האא | נתה |
| ייז | רהע | וזעם | אני | מנד | כוק | להוז | יוזו |
| מיה | עשל | ערי | סאל | ילה | וול | מיכ | ההה |
| פוי | מבה | נית | ננא | עמם | הוזש | דני | והו |
| מוזי | ענו | יהה | ומב | מצר | הרוז | ייל | גמם |
| מום | היי | יבמ | ראה | וזבו | איע | מנק | דמב |

PART THREE

AUTHOR'S NOTE

As I look back on the unfolding of *The 72 Names of God*, I know that I did not write this book. Rather, these powerful life-enhancing tools had to be made available to people now, and I happened to be in the right place at the right time.

According to the ancient Kabbalists, there are particular windows of time when global miracles can happen and profound aspects of wisdom can be revealed for the betterment of humankind. This is just such a time, and it provides a tremendous opportunity for those whose destiny it is to be part of it. I am eternally grateful for being part of the 72 Names of God as they reveal themselves to the world.

The Names have such a rich history, such diversity and beauty that it could take a lifetime to discover all their significance and power. The more research I did, the more I uncovered. I felt like a spiritual archaeologist on the dig of a lifetime. With each exploratory step forward, I was led into a vast dimension of wisdom, rich with history.

My first real inspiration to do something with the Names came in late February of 1991. My father had returned from Rabat, Morocco, where he had met with the late king of Morocco to promote a peaceful resolution to the Gulf War. The meeting had been arranged by one of the students of The Kabbalah Centre who was a friend of the king.

While in Morocco my father and the king spent many private hours together sharing stories and insights, as great leaders will do, once they have become friends.

One evening, the king took my father to his private office and shared with him a special gift given to him by his father. "Keep this with you at all times," the king's father had said to him. "It will protect you." On a piece of cherished parchment were several of the 72 Names.

When my father told me this story I was blown away. This tool, which I had grown up with and had taken perhaps a little lightly, had crossed borders, cultures, religions, and was still treasured as a tremendous secret weapon.

I knew then that I had to take part in bringing this wisdom to as many people as possible.

You will notice when you review the 72 Names that several of the Names appear twice, for example, לאו is repeated on pages 71 and 83. I was unable to discover why. As my research into the 72 Names continues, I will be placing new insights on the website, which can be reached at www.72.com. For example, a really useful aspect of the Names that I was not able to include in this book was the formula for discovering that Name of the 72 that has special significance for you. By referring to your birth date and hour you can calculate this Name, which helps you when you need direction, or when you are coping with challenges that are specific to your own correction, your purpose in this world.

When you log on to the website, look for the Personal 72 Name designation on the navigation bar and we will help you to figure out which of the 72 Names has this special impact on your destiny. Enjoy!

# INDEX

LIST OF 72 NAMES (TRANSLITERATIONS)

| 01 | וָהוּ | VAV HEY VAV | (Time Travel) |
| 02 | יְלִי | YUD LAMED YUD | (Recapturing the Sparks) |
| 03 | סִיט | SAMECH YUD TET | (Miracle Making) |
| 04 | עֶלֶם | AYIN LAMED MEM | (Eliminating Negative Thoughts) |
| 05 | מֲהַשׁ | MEM HEY SHIN | (Healing) |
| 06 | לֶלֵה | LAMED LAMED HEY | (Dream State) |
| 07 | אַכָא | ALEPH KAF ALEPH | (DNA of the Soul) |
| 08 | כַהַת | KAF HEY TAV | (Defusing Negative Energy and Stress) |
| 09 | הֵזִי | HEY ZAYIN YUD | (Angelic Influences) |
| 10 | אֶלֶד | ALEPH LAMED DALED | (Looks Can Kill) |
| 11 | לָאו | LAMED ALEPH VAV | (Banishing the Remnants of Evil) |
| 12 | הֵהַע | HEY HEY AYIN | (Unconditional Love) |
| 13 | יֵזֶל | YUD ZAYIN LAMED | (Heaven on Earth) |
| 14 | מֵבַה | MEM BET HEY | (Farewell to Arms) |
| 15 | הָרִי | HEY RESH YUD | (Long-Range Vision) |
| 16 | הַקֶם | HEY KUF MEM | (Dumping Depression) |
| 17 | לָאו | LAMED ALEPH VAV | (Great Escape) |
| 18 | כֶלִי | KAF LAMED YUD | (Fertility) |
| 19 | לוֵו | LAMED VAV VAV | (Dialing God) |
| 20 | פֶהֵל | PEY HEY LAMED | (Victory Over Addictions) |
| 21 | נֶלֶך | NUN LAMED KAF | (Eradicate Plague) |
| 22 | יִיִי | YUD YUD YUD | (Stop Fatal Attraction) |
| 23 | מֶלֵה | MEM LAMED HEY | (Sharing the Flame) |
| 24 | וֶהֵו | CHET HEY VAV | (Jealousy) |
| 25 | נֵתֵה | NUN TAV HEY | (Speak Your Mind) |

| 26 | הֹאא | HEY ALEPH ALEPH | (Order from Chaos) |
| 27 | ירת | YUD RESH TAV | (Silent Partner) |
| 28 | שׂאה | SHIN ALEPH HEY | (Soul Mate) |
| 29 | רֹיֹי | RESH YUD YUD | (Removing Hatred) |
| 30 | אֹוֹם | ALEPH VAV MEM | (Building Bridges) |
| 31 | לכב | LAMED KAF BET | (Finish What You Start) |
| 32 | וֹשֹׁר | VAV SHIN RESH | (Memories) |
| 33 | יֹוֹו | YUD CHET VAV | (Revealing the Dark Side) |
| 34 | לֹהֹוֹ | LAMED HEY CHET | (Forget Thyself) |
| 35 | כֹוֹק | KAF VAV KUF | (Sexual Energy) |
| 36 | מֹנֹד | MEM NUN DALED | (Fear(less)) |
| 37 | אֹנֹי | ALEPH NUN YUD | (The Big Picture) |
| 38 | וֹעֹם | CHET AYIN MEM | (Circuitry) |
| 39 | רֹהֹע | RESH HEY AYIN | (Diamond in the Rough) |
| 40 | יֹיֹז | YUD YUD ZAYIN | (Speaking the Right Words) |
| 41 | הֹהֹה | HEY HEY HEY | (Self-Esteem) |
| 42 | מֹיֹכ | MEM YUD KAF | (Revealing the Concealed) |
| 43 | וֹוֹל | VAV VAV LAMED | (Defying Gravity) |
| 44 | יֹלֹה | YUD LAMED HEY | (Sweetening Judgement) |
| 45 | סֹאֹל | SAMECH ALEPH LAMED | (The Power of Prosperity) |
| 46 | עֹרֹי | AYIN RESH YUD | (Absolute Certainty) |
| 47 | עֹשֹׂל | AYIN SHIN LAMED | (Global Transformation) |
| 48 | מֹיֹה | MEM YUD HEY | (Unity) |
| 49 | וֹהֹו | VAV HEY VAV | (Happiness) |
| 50 | דֹנֹי | DALED NUN YUD | (Enough Is Never Enough) |

| | | | |
|---|---|---|---|
| 51 | הֹוֹשֵׁי | HEY CHET SHIN | (No Guilt) |
| 52 | עֹמֶם | AYIN MEM MEM | (Passion) |
| 53 | נֹנֵא | NUN NUN ALEPH | (No Agenda) |
| 54 | נֵית | NUN YUD TAV | (The Death of Death) |
| 55 | מֹבֹה | MEM BET HEY | (Thought into Action) |
| 56 | פֹוִי | PEY VAV YUD | (Dispelling Anger) |
| 57 | נֹמֵם | NUN MEM MEM | (Listening to Your Soul) |
| 58 | יֵיֹל | YUD YUD LAMED | (Letting Go) |
| 59 | הֹרֹח | HEY RESH CHET | (Umbilical Cord) |
| 60 | מֹצֹר | MEM ZADIK RESH | (Freedom) |
| 61 | וֹמֹב | VAV MEM BET | (Water) |
| 62 | יֹהֹה | YUD HEY HEY | (Parent—Teacher, Not Preacher) |
| 63 | עֹנֹו | AYIN NUN VAV | (Appreciation) |
| 64 | מֹחֹי | MEM CHET YUD | (Casting Yourself in a Favorable Light) |
| 65 | דֹמֹב | DALED MEM BET | (Fear of God) |
| 66 | מֹנֹק | MEM NUN KUF | (Accountability) |
| 67 | אִיֹע | ALEPH YUD AYIN | (Great Expectations) |
| 68 | וֹזֹבֹו | CHET BET VAV | (Contacting Departed Souls) |
| 69 | רֹאֹה | RESH ALEPH HEY | (Lost and Found) |
| 70 | יֹבֹמֹ | YUD BET MEM | (Recognizing Design Beneath Disorder) |
| 71 | הֹיֹי | HEY YUD YUD | (Prophecy and Parallel Universes) |
| 72 | מֹוֹם | MEM VAV MEM | (Spiritual Cleansing) |

## ADDITIONAL 72 NAMES PRODUCTS

### Lamed Aleph Vav
### T-Shirt

According to Kabbalah, it is the ego, the "me, me, me," that holds us back from our potential. Get rid of that filter, and the world looks completely different. The letters Lamed Aleph Vav have the power to squash your ego. Just close your eyes and visualize them, and enjoy the natural high. There is no limit to what you can achieve—love, money, health, happiness—when your ego is out of the way.

Available in white or black, long sleeve, short sleeve or tank, the Lamed Aleph Vav t-shirt plays on the ultimate paradox: It helps you destroy your ego while its fitted styling flatters you.

### Aleph Lamed Daled
### Red String Protection

Kabbalists attribute much of everyday misfortunes to the evil eye—the negative glances and resentful looks we receive from people harboring destructive feelings toward us.

The three-letter sequence of the Aleph Lamed Daled is one of several safeguards including the red string that, according to Kabbalah, offers protection from looks of envy and the mean-spirited intentions of others.

Used for centuries by the Kabbalists, the red string connects us to Rachel the Matriarch, who represents the aspect of protection in the physical realm. Her greatest desire and purpose in life was to protect and defend all of her children from evil. That is why she evokes the element of protection from the universe. Each piece of red string produced by The Kabbalah Centre is taken to Rachel's tomb in Israel, and with the power of the Aleph Lamed Daled, it is imbued with the essence of protection. The red string is worn on the left wrist, the receiving side of the body and soul, sealing protective energy within while intercepting negative influences that exist.

## Mem Vav Mem
## Spiritual Cleansing Sage

You'd be amazed if you could see the entities that may be lingering around your home or clinging to your physical body! Negative actions leave behind a residue that can clutter up your emotional and physical life.

בום has the power to cleanse your body and your environment. Used in combination with sage, an herb known through the ages for its cleansing properties, this potent duo absorbs negativity and enhances the flow of life as it drives away any negative forces and tensions that can give rise to misfortune.

## 72 Names of God DVD

In this remarkable DVD, Kabbalist Yehuda Berg expounds upon the knowledge he reveals in his best selling book, *The 72 Names of God*. In his clear, engaging style, Yehuda speaks about the most effective ways to meditate with the Names, and what to expect in the process.

He offers a lesson for each Name and, more importantly, how to apply these 72 direct lines to God to help you in the struggles of everyday life: find your soul mate, remove obstacles, enhance moment-to-moment experiences, financial prosperity, replace conflict with unity.

With his gift for story telling, Yehuda shares the poignant stories and experiences of those who have made the impossible possible using the Names.

Special guest appearances add mystery and charm to this illuminating production. Get your copy today and hear the secrets directly from the source.

## 72 Names of God Wall Chart

Dealing with a difficult person or situation, having doubts, struggling with your thoughts? Whatever the situation, there is a Name that can give you your power back. With *The 72 Names of God Wall Chart*, you can access this ancient technology on your wall, desk, dashboard, or wherever you need it.

The graphics and information printed on this chart are organized and presented in an easy to use format. After your first use, you will wonder how you ever got along without it.

## 72 Names of God Meditation Deck

The convenient set of *The 72 Names of God Meditation Deck* was created for you to carry and use whenever you need them, at any moment and in any situation you may face. They are an effective way to keep and use the Names at all times.

Each beautifully designed meditation card displays the Name, a life-changing affirmation, and the same compelling graphics found in the book.

Using them can lead you towards self-improvement, increased joy, greater mental clarity and physical energy, rejuvenation of passion, and so much more.

Whether at home, on the train, or in the office, use your 72 Names to make the impossible possible. Please feel free to write us with any experiences you wish to share as a result of using *The 72 Names of God*, at www.72.com.

## More from Yehuda Berg
### *The Power of Kabbalah*

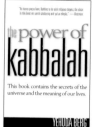

Imagine your life filled with unending joy, purpose, and contentment. Imagine your days infused with pure insight and energy. This is *The Power of Kabbalah*. It is the path from the momentary pleasure that most of us settle for, to the lasting fulfillment that is yours to claim. Your deepest desires *are* waiting to be realized. But they are not limited to the temporary rush from closing a business deal, the short-term high from drugs, or a passionate sexual relationship that lasts only a few short months.

Wouldn't you like to experience a lasting sense of wholeness and peace that is unshakable, no matter what may be happening around you? Complete fulfillment is the promise of Kabbalah. Within these pages, you will learn how to look at and navigate through life in a whole new way. You will understand your purpose and how to receive the abundant gifts waiting for you. By making a critical transformation from a reactive to a proactive being, you will increase your creative energy, get control of your life, and enjoy new spiritual levels of existence. Kabbalah's ancient teaching is rooted in the perfect union of the physical and spiritual laws already at work in your life. Get ready to experience this exciting realm of awareness, meaning, and joy.

The wonder and wisdom of Kabbalah has influenced the world's leading spiritual, philosophical, religious, and scientific minds. Until today, however, it was hidden away in ancient texts, available only to scholars who knew where to look. Now after many centuries, *The Power of Kabbalah* resides right here in this one remarkable book. Here, at long last is the complete and simple path—actions you can take right now to create the life you desire and deserve.

## MORE PRODUCTS THAT CAN HELP YOU BRING THE WISDOM OF KABBALAH INTO YOUR LIFE

### *The Secret*
### By Michael Berg

Like a jewel that has been painstakingly cut and polished, *The Secret* reveals life's essence in its most concise and powerful form. Michael Berg begins by showing you how our everyday understanding of our purpose in the world is literally backwards. Whenever there is pain in our lives, indeed whenever there is anything less than complete joy and fulfillment, this basic misunderstanding is the reason.

### *The Essential Zohar*
### By Rav Berg

The Zohar has traditionally been known as the world's most esoteric and profound spiritual document, but Rav Berg has dedicated his life to making this wisdom universally available. The vast wisdom and Light of The Zohar came into being as a gift to all humanity, and *The Essential Zohar* at last explains that gift to the world.

## AUDIO RESOURCES

### *The Power of Kabbalah* Tape Series

*The Power of Kabbalah* is nothing less than a user's guide to the universe. Move beyond where you are right now to where you truly want to be—emotionally, spiritually, creatively. This exciting tape series brings you the ancient, authentic teaching of Kabbalah in a powerful, practical audio format.

### *Creating Miracles in Your Life*

We're used to thinking of a miracle as something that happens at the whim of God. But the Kabbalists have long taught that the true power to create miracles is present in each and every one of us—if only we can learn to access that power and put it into practice. This inspiring tape series shows how to do exactly that. Order it now, and enter the zone of the miraculous!

## The Zohar

*Bringing The Zohar from near oblivion to wide accessibility has taken many decades. It is an achievement of which we are truly proud and grateful.*
—Michael Berg

Composed more than 2,000 years ago, The Zohar is a set of 22 books, a commentary on biblical and spiritual matters in the form of conversations among spiritual masters. But to describe The Zohar only in physical terms is hugely misleading. In truth, The Zohar is nothing less than a powerful tool for achieving the most important purposes of our lives. It was given to all humankind by the Creator to bring us protection, to connect us with the Creator's Light, and ultimately to fulfill our birthright of true spiritual transformation.

Eighty years ago, when The Kabbalah Centre was founded, The Zohar had virtually disappeared from the world. Few people in the general population had ever heard of it. Whoever might wish to read it—in any country, in any language, at any price—faced a long and futile search.

Today all this has changed. Through the work of The Kabbalah Centre and the editorial efforts of Michael Berg, The Zohar is now being brought to the world, not only in the original Aramaic language, but also in English.

The new English Zohar provides everything for connecting to this sacred text on all levels: the original Aramaic text for scanning; an English translation; and clear, concise commentary for study and learning.

Since its founding, The Kabbalah Centre has had a single mission: to improve and transform people's lives by bringing the power and wisdom of Kabbalah to all who wish to partake of it.

Through the lifelong efforts of Rav Berg, his wife Karen, and the great spiritual lineage of which they are part, an astonishing 3.5 million people around the world have already been touched by the powerful teachings of Kabbalah. And each year, the numbers are growing!

As the leading source of Kabbalistic wisdom with 50 locations around the world, The Kabbalah Centre offers you a wealth of resources, including:

- The English Zohar, the first-ever comprehensive English translation of the foundation of Kabbalistic wisdom. In 22 beautifully bound volumes, this edition includes the full Aramaic text, the English translation, and detailed commentary, making this once-inaccessible text understandable to all.

- A full schedule of workshops, lectures, and evening classes for students at all levels of knowledge and experience.

- CDs, audio and videotapes, and books in English and ten other languages.

- One of the Internet's most exciting and comprehensive websites— **www.kabbalah.com**—which receives more than 100,000 visitors each month.

- A constantly expanding list of events and publications to help you live *The Secret* and other teachings of Kabbalah with greater understanding and excitement.

Discover why The Kabbalah Centre is one of the world's fastest growing spiritual organizations. Our sole purpose is to improve people's lives through the teachings of Kabbalah. Let us show you what Kabbalah can do for you!

Every Kabbalah Centre location hosts free introductory lectures. For more information on Kabbalah, or on these and other products and services available, call 1-800-Kabbalah.

If you want more information on *The 72 Names* and would like to share your ideas and experiences with others, take advantage of *The 72 Names* book clubs located throughout the world, or to start your own, call 877-KCLASSES or visit our website at www.72.com.

### *FREE* 72 NAMES CONSULTATION

**Call 1-800-KABBALAH for a FREE 10 minute personal consultation with a highly trained 72 Names teacher. Find out exactly how the 72 Names can help you with the issues you're facing in your life right now!**

When the time is ripe, true soul mates find one another, even if they are worlds apart. May the power of *The 72 Names of God* bring Nachshon ben Abraham his other half. And together may they strengthen the force of peace throughout the world.